Slightly Below the

RAF Waddi

This book is dedicated to all who have served
their country at RAF Waddington

First published in Great Britain in 2013
by Fox 3 Publishing
York
YO32 3QX (69)

Printed in Great Britain by
Inc Dot Design and Print
Inc Dot House
Seafire Close
Clifton Moor
York YO30 4UU

A catalogue record for this book is available from
The British Library

ISBN 978-0-9566319-2-3

The Airman's Prayer

If I climb up into heaven, thou art there

If I go down to hell, thou art there also

If I take the wings of the morning

And remain in the uttermost parts of the sea

Even there also shall thy hand lead me

And thy right hand shall hold me

The above prayer is inscribed upon the chapel windows of the Air Forces Memorial at Runnymede

Introduction

Near to most RAF stations, past and present, there are nominated burial sites for airmen and airwomen who die in service. Some die in tragic circumstances, often in connection with flying. Others die from natural causes, road accidents and the like. All that is seen by the casual observer are a number of neatly lined up gravestones showing just the name of the person buried and the date they died. Nothing is shown as to how or why they died and that is the reason for our book.

We have tried to investigate each serviceman or woman's death with the help of official records and in some cases the families and friends of the deceased. We try to produce a well researched, accurate account of the deaths whilst balancing the sensitivities of family, friends and sometimes the RAF itself. Each person buried at Waddington has a story to tell. We hope you enjoy reading their stories and in that way they will never be forgotten.

Waddington War Memorial adjacent to St Michael's Churchyard.

Most of the home based military burials for RAF Waddington lie in the churchyard of St Michael's Church, High Street, Waddington or in the public cemetery near the station gates, although others lie in churchyards outside the village such as Lincoln and Nettleham.

In most towns and villages a War Memorial exists to commemorate the local people lost in the First and Second World Wars. The War Memorial for Waddington is just outside the churchyard and was unveiled on 9th November 2003. It replaced the previous one which was destroyed when the church was bombed by the German Luftwaffe on 8th May 1941. The metal railings are inscribed 'Lest we forget' and the York granite stone bears the words 'In memory of Waddington men and women who gave their lives during conflicts for our country.'

Adjacent to the memorial stone is an imposing clock tower which commemorates the members of No 463 and No 467 Squadrons of the Royal Australian Air Force who were based at Waddington and gave their lives in World War 2. The clock was dedicated on 10th May 1987.

Father Gerry Aspinall leads the dedication service for the Memorial Clock in 1987 during a re-union for 463 and 467 Squadrons. Pictured in the front row left to right are: Mr Healey, Colin Cole, Group Captain Tait, Group Captain McAlister, Mrs Morphen, The Honourable Douglas McLelland (Australian High Commissioner), Mrs McLelland and Group Captain Bonnor .

4

The History of RAF Waddington

Waddington is one of the oldest military airfields in Lincolnshire on a similar footing to its near and equally famous neighbour RAF Scampton. It came into use with the Royal Flying Corps (The predecessor of the Royal Air Force) in 1916. It was basically an area of grazing land south of Lincoln made ready for pilot training squadrons of 27 Training Wing.

Top: 27 Wing at Waddington 4th September 1917. Bottom: HQ Staff of 27 Wing

27 Wing HQ Staff at Waddington

The Royal Air Force Museum at Hendon write up this period as follows: "With the outbreak of the First World War in August 1914 it was clear that the RFC would have to expand if it were to serve the army in France and replace its own casualties, so new training units were opened. The quality of instructors varied and many of the aircraft used were unsuitable. Accidents were common and for most of the war casualties at training units were greater than losses in action.

In early 1916 the RFC began regulating the training standards and pupils were expected to fly at least 15 hours solo. Unfortunately the demands for pilots at the front meant that students often received insufficient training and arrived at the front unprepared for combat. Partly because of this casualties rose sharply and by the Spring of 1917 the life expectancy of a new pilot could be measured in weeks".

Gradually the situation improved and the Training Brigade was formed, staffed by veterans. This together with the introduction of a new style of training (The Gosport System) helped the RFC turn out large numbers of capable combat pilots and reduce accidents. When the RAF was formed on 1st April 1918 there were over 100 training squadrons with some 7000 aircraft. By the Armistice in November 1918 the flying course was of eleven months duration with pupils receiving instruction in all aspects of air fighting and an average of 50 hours solo flying.

The picture opposite shows a typical early accident at Waddington with the original caption below it telling its own story.

In July 1918 Waddington became 48 Training Depot Station flying a variety of aircraft types until the First World War came to an end.

In 1919 the station closed but re-opened in October 1926 when 503 Squadron was formed to fly Fairy Fawn light bombers, later changing to Hyderabad, Hart and later Hind aircraft.

THE PILOT WAS FOUND SITTING BY THE TREE SMOKING WHILE FUEL DRIPPED FROM HIS A/C

The hangar roof seems to have been an alternative landing site for this Farman MF 11 Shorthorn.

A DH 6, built by Ransomes, Sims and Jeffries crashes into the WAAF Hut at Waddington

Waddington's buildings seemed to attract its aircraft

After the First World War there was a dramatic reduction for the RAF in both manpower and aircraft. The government foresaw no further possibility of war through the 1920's so little happened in the way of funding for the RAF because of the vast expense of the war.

By the early 1930's however, it was clear that Germany was expanding and could offer a threat again. Following the break up of disarmament talks it was in 1935 that the government set about an RAF Expansion programme. The then Prime Minister, Stanley Baldwin said "In air strength and air power this country shall no longer be in a position inferior to any country within striking distance of our shores"

In an original, multi million pound five year plan, airfields were modernised, new ones were built and new aircraft were ordered and produced. Airfields such as Waddington were to see firmer grass runways and extensive building to provide permanent barracks, hangars and technical facilities, all to laid down common specifications. The emphasis was on bombers such as the Whitley, Wellington, Hampden, Blenheim and Battle. In 1936 though specifications were put to the aircraft industry that later resulted in the Short Stirling, the first four engine bomber.

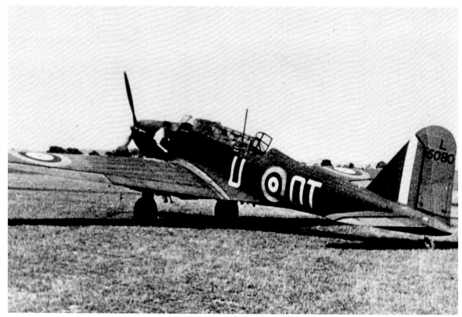

Fairey Battle L5080 of 142 Squadron at Waddington in 1941

On completion of the building works the station came under the control of Bomber Command (5 Group) and two new squadrons were to take up residence in May 1937. Both 50 and 110 Squadrons, still flying the Hind were joined a month later by 44 Squadron who flew the same aircraft. In December 1937, 44 Squadron were re-equipped with the Blenheim and a month later 110 Squadron followed suit but moved out in May 1939.

44 Squadron Blenheims over Lincolnshire

10

A pair of 50 Squadron Hampdens

50 Squadron traded in its Hinds for the Hampden in December 1938 and two months later 44 Squadron were also re-equipped with the Hampden.

Waddington's Hampdens saw action from the first day of the Second World War. On that first day, nine aircraft were involved in searching for enemy naval action in the area of Heligoland (In the North Sea off the coast of Germany).

50 Squadron moved out in July 1940, but 44 Squadron was to fly its aircraft from Waddington until the airfield closed to have concrete runways laid in May 1943. Meanwhile 207 Squadron was formed at Waddington in November 1940 and was to receive the first Avro Manchester heavy bomber and take it to war.

One of 207 Squadron's first Manchesters to arrive at Waddington

Their first operational mission was to attack the docks at Brest on the night of February 24th 1941. No aircraft were lost. 207 Squadron moved out of Waddington in November 1941.

In December 1941 the Canadians arrived at Waddington when 420 Squadron was formed to fly Hampdens. Later in the same month their predecessors, 44 Squadron became the first unit to receive the new Avro Lancaster which they took into action for the first time on 10th March 1942 on a mission to Essen. Shortly afterwards, on the night of 17th April 1942, 44 Squadron and 97 Squadron from nearby Woodhall Spa joined forces when their Lancasters went on a mission to bomb the MAN diesel works in Augsburg which

Two groups at Waddington in front of their Hampden bomber. Top picture is not verified other than marked as "Waddington aircrew". Bottom picture is 50 Squadron in 1940.

Squadron Leader Nettleton V C

made diesel engines for submarines. On this rare daylight raid, Squadron Leader John Nettleton's actions were so heroic that he was awarded the Victoria Cross. The citation for his award appears below and describes the mission in detail.

Five of the six aircraft from 44 Squadron were shot down by either flak or fighters, as were two from 97 Squadron, with Nettleton being the only one to make it back to base from 44 Squadron.

The Squadron lost 24 aircrew killed with 11 more being taken prisoner of war. 97 Squadron lost two of their aircraft with 13 aircrew killed and one taken prisoner of war. A drawing of the attack appears overleaf. John Nettleton later died on operations on 13th July 1943. His citation published in the London Gazette on 28th April 1942 reads as follows:

The KING has been graciously pleased to confer the VICTORIA CROSS on the under mentioned officer in recognition of most conspicuous bravery

Acting Squadron Leader John Dering Nettleton (41452), No. 44 (Rhodesia) Squadron.

Squadron Leader Nettleton was the leader of one of two formations of six Lancaster heavy bombers detailed to deliver a low-level attack in daylight on the diesel engine factory at Augsburg in Southern Germany on April 17th 1942. The enterprise was daring, the target of high military importance. To reach it and get back, some 1,000 miles had to be flown over hostile territory.
Soon after crossing into enemy territory his formation was engaged by 25 to 30 fighters. A running fight ensued. His rear guns went out of action. One by one the aircraft of his formation were shot down until in the end only his and one other remained. The fighters were shaken off but the target was still far distant. There was formidable resistance to be faced.
With great spirit and almost defenceless, he held his two remaining aircraft on their perilous course and after a long and arduous flight, mostly at only 50 feet above the ground, he brought them to Augsburg. Here anti-aircraft fire of great intensity and accuracy was encountered. The two aircraft came low over the roof tops. Though fired at from point blank range, they stayed the course to drop their bombs true on the target. The second aircraft, hit by flak, burst into flames and crash-landed. The leading aircraft, though riddled with holes, flew safely back to base, the only one of the six to return.
Squadron Leader Nettleton, who has successfully undertaken many other hazardous operations, displayed unflinching determination as well as leadership and valour of the highest order

Drawing by an unknown artist showing Squadron Leader John Nettleton earning his Victoria Cross.

44 and 420 Squadrons continued to take the fight to the enemy with 420 Squadron still flying the Hampden, one of the last units in Bomber Command to do so until it moved out of Waddington in August 1942 to be replaced by 9 Squadron.

Both 9 and 44 Squadrons equipped with the Lancaster continued to mount operations from Waddington until the airfield was closed in May 1943 to build concrete runways. Both squadrons left for other airfields.

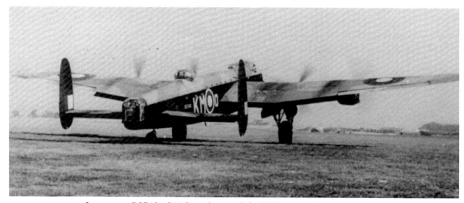

Lancaster R5740 of 44 Squadron in July 1942 - note the grass runways

14

A Lancaster safely airborne off Waddington's new concrete runway post October 1943.

During the war Waddington lost more bombers on operations than any other Bomber Command station, a total of 345 (103 Hampdens, 15 Manchesters and 227 Lancasters).

The new runways were laid and some newly built accommodation allowed the station to cater for 2,085 males and 390 females and it re-opened for flying in October 1943. The new occupants were the Australians in the form of 463 and 467 Squadrons. These two squadrons stayed at Waddington until after VE Day flying Lancasters. 467 Squadron moved out in June 1945 with 463 Squadron moving out a month later.

Over the next eight years several squadrons were based at Waddington including 12, 57 and 61 all flying the Lincoln until in mid 1953 the airfield was closed again, this time for 2 years to revamp buildings and runways to accommodate the new generation of very heavy aircraft.

A Waddington based Lincoln flies over the City of the same name

In 1955 the shiny new station accepted its first very heavy bombers when 21 and 27 Squadrons arrived with their Canberra aircraft. These two squadrons were disbanded in May 1957 when Waddington became the home of the Vulcan Bomber and the first Vulcan Squadron took up residence. This was 83 Squadron which had been re-formed for the task. In August 1960 a re-formed 44 Squadron returned to Waddington taking over from 83 Squadron who left for nearby RAF Scampton.

A Vulcan aircraft captain checks out the Form 700 (Servicing Record) with the crew chief prior to flight. The other four crew members stand near the hatch ready to board

By 1961, 44, 50 and 101 Squadrons were based at Waddington all flying the Vulcan. These aircraft were essential as part of the British nuclear deterrent, previously the responsibility of RAF units using the American Thor ballistic missiles from September 1958 until the government announced it would transfer the deterrent to air and submarine assets in 1960.

The deterrent was held by the Vulcan squadrons based at several locations including Waddington until the responsibility was passed in full to the Royal Navy and its Polaris submarines on 30th June 1969. At it's peak in 1961 the V Force (Vulcan, Victor and Valiant) had 164 V bombers in 17 squadrons.

Refuelling a Vulcan B1 at Waddington at night

When the RAF decided to change the role of the Vulcan from high level bombing to low level bombing they changed the colour scheme from anti-flash white to camouflage. Above Vulcan B2 XM649 flies low level over the Lincolnshire countryside.

In 1982 just as the Vulcan was being withdrawn from service Argentinean armed forces attacked the Falkland Islands. A task force was sent down by Prime Minister Margaret Thatcher to re-take the islands, albeit they were 8000 miles away from England. It was decided that a long range mission to drop bombs on the Island's airfield which was being used by the attackers would send a strong message about RAF capabilities, frustrating the enemy and forcing their thoughts to their air assets protecting their main cities as opposed to attacking the Task Force.

The only suitable aircraft was the Vulcan, which would need to be modified to carry wing mounted weapons and to drop conventional iron bombs (No different to the Lancasters in World War Two). In what was known as Operation Black Buck each mission was an 8000 mile round trip from Ascension Island to the Falklands taking 16 hours and involving the support of 13 tankers. Of the planned seven, five of these attacks were successfully carried out. The first involved Waddington Vulcan XM607 which is now the Gate Guardian at RAF Waddington. It also flew the second and last sortie.

Waddington Vulcan XM597 which was modified to carry Shrike missiles to attack enemy radar on the Falkland Islands. It took part in the Black Buck 4 mission on 28th May 1982 to do exactly that, but the mission was aborted, as whilst refuelling en route the probe snapped off, leaving them without enough fuel to return to Ascension Island. The aircraft diverted to Rio de Janeiro in Brazil and following a May Day call was allowed to land (With not enough fuel left to do a circuit of the airfield first). It gained world wide attention from the media when the Brazilian authorities impounded it, but was released on 10th June. It now resides at East Fortune Air Museum.

Following the withdrawal of the Vulcan, RAF Waddington saw the arrival of 8 Squadron and their Boeing E-3D Airborne Early Warning (AEW) aircraft known in the RAF as the Sentry AEW Mk 1. The squadron has been based at Waddington since 1991 and at the time of writing (2013) it is still in residence. The squadron of over 100 aircrew provides airborne early warning and command and control functions and has been involved in many recent conflicts. It regularly operates all over the world.

One of 8 Squadron's Sentry aircraft.

51 Squadron, also currently in residence at Waddington arrived in 1995 from RAF Wyton with its Nimrod R1 aircraft operating in a signals, intelligence gathering role. The Nimrod was phased out of service by 28th June 2011 to be replaced in 2014 by the Boeing 135V/W Rivet Joint aircraft designed to carry out very sophisticated signals / intelligence gathering roles. Crews are currently flying this aircraft having worked up in America.

Boeing 135V/W Rivet Joint

The other major squadron in current residence at Waddington is 5 (AC) Squadron, the AC standing for Army Co-operation. This squadron flies the ASTOR (Airborne Stand Off Radar) system which is based on the Bombardier Global Express long range business jet - heavily modified for its RAF role where it is named the Sentinel R Mk 1. The R recognises its Reconnaissance role. The squadron was re-formed at Waddington on 1st April 2004 with its first aircraft arriving in 2007.

The squadron has a formidable capability with this aircraft which uses cutting edge technology for military intelligence, surveillance and reconnaissance. As a jointly managed RAF Squadron, the composition of the unit is like no other, with almost 300 personnel split between army, RAF and civilians, making it one of the biggest flying squadrons.

One of 5 (AC) Squadron's Sentinel aircraft

RAF Waddington has other ground assets and specialities and together with the highly technical aerial assets they make the station one of the busiest and diverse in the Royal Air Force.

Service burials and Grave Markers

Before World War One the burying of the deceased service man was traditionally the responsibility of the Ship or Regiment to which they belonged. No formal assistance was offered by what was then the Admiralty or War Office. Only a few that were buried in a military cemetery are maintained by what is now the Ministry of Defence (MOD)

During World War One there was no repatriation for those killed abroad and they were buried where they fell or where they died in the various levels of medical care. Such were the numbers of dead that the Imperial War Graves Commission (later re-named as the Commonwealth War Graves Commission) was established in 1917 by Royal Charter. They built cemeteries, designed by the best architects of the time, all around the battlefields. Bodies were laid to rest and graves were marked with a standard stone grave marker showing generally the crest of the Service or Regiment, the rank and name of the deceased and the date of death.

The relatives of those who died on home soil, often whilst training, in accidents or hospitals were offered service burials with similar headstones but possibly not such splendid settings of cemetery, or private family burial. Many First World War headstones for such burials can be found scattered in cemeteries or churchyards around the country. In between the First and Second World Wars responsibility went back to as it had been before 1914 with arrangements being made by Ships, Regiments and units, generally without central assistance.

During the Second World War the Imperial War Graves Commission again took on the role of burying the dead and maintaining their graves in perpetuity. Once again there was no repatriation and servicemen and women were buried where they fought and fell so they could be honoured together.

Unlike the First World War, which was intense in particular areas with the high death toll producing large cemeteries, the Second World War was faster moving over land and featured many more casualties from airborne offensives. Where a World War One Imperial War Graves Cemetery existed near where a person died they would often be buried there. Others would be buried in new cemeteries built after the war.

Homeland burials, particularly those for RAF personnel, became quite complicated. Pre 1943 most RAF Stations had a local plot of land - often in a churchyard or local public cemetery where service personnel could be buried.

Whereas many families took the option offered of a private family burial at the deceased's home town, many did take the other option of a Service burial.

Interestingly, where a member of aircrew died whilst involved in an air crash in England on the way to or from operations or in a training accident away from their home station and a service funeral was elected, they would mostly be buried at the RAF site nearest to where they crashed as opposed to a return to home station. Many Commonwealth aircrew were killed in similar ways and were not repatriated to their own countries, so they were buried in exactly the same way, but without the option of a family burial.

Established from 1943, with local cemeteries and burial places filling up, Service burials took place in regional military cemeteries, often near military hospitals such as Harrogate (Stonefall) Cemetery in Yorkshire, a Commonwealth War Graves Commission site, where there are 954 Air Force Second World War burials,665 of whom are Canadian.

Airmen of the RAF and Commonwealth Air Forces who flew from bases in the United Kingdom, North or Western Europe, who were lost without trace, whether this be on operations or whilst training and therefore have no known grave, are commemorated on The Air Forces Memorial at Runnymede by name. There are 20,315 names on the Memorial. in perpetuity.

The Air Forces Memorial at Runnymede

There was an extension to the end of each of the two war dates to allow for deaths from war injuries etc. to be buried by the Imperial War Graves Commission. Up to 31st August 1921 for the First World War and 31st December 1947 for the Second World War. From 1st January 1948, Ministry of Defence (MOD) policy was, that if a member of the Armed Forces died in service, their next of kin would be offered a Service funeral and an official headstone to be maintained at public expense in perpetuity. There was no repatriation for those who died outside of the United Kingdom, so they were buried locally or could be repatriated and buried at private expense with a private funeral.

However, in 1963 the policy of non repatriation changed whereby the next of kin of service personnel or accompanying dependants dying in North West Europe were offered either repatriation and burial at public expense or the cost of two relatives travelling to attend the funeral service overseas. In 1967 this changed to include the rest of the world.

The MOD maintain the graves and headstones of those who had a Service funeral and a Service headstone in perpetuity, but where a private funeral or where the next of kin chose a non standard headstone following a Service funeral, the graves are maintained privately and the MOD has no responsibility for them.

Headstones are most easily identified by the shape of the top: Below left: left a typical mid-wars headstone, middle a standard Commonwealth War Graves Commission headstone and right the standard post war headstone.

St Michael's Churchyard

As you have read, the history of RAF Waddington dates back to the First World War through to the present day. The cemetery in St Michael's Churchyard reflects that history up to December 1958.

Many of the Service burials are of airmen who died during the Second World War and fifteen are post that war. There are also two burials of servicemen from the First World War, Private John William Clarkson of the North Staffordshire Regiment and Second Lieutenant Craig Royston Marks of the Royal Flying Corps.

Details are shown of each burial in date order, headed by the name and rank of the individual and the date of death. The circumstances of their death and others who may have died alongside them are shown in the text.

Second Lieutenant Craig Royston Marks

Royal Flying Corps

Died 3rd May 1917

Second Lieutenant Marks was a Canadian serving with the Royal Flying Corps. He was training to be a pilot with 47 Training Wing at Waddington.

A landmark in any pilot's career is the first time they are sent to fly an aeroplane solo. It comes as a surprise to most that this generally occurred after just a few hours flying training. The first flight is a simple circuit of the airfield and usually only last a few minutes. For Second Lieutenant Marks, his first solo flight was to take place in a Maurice Farman Shorthorn (A7094) of 47 (Training) Squadron. At first, all went well, he made a good take-off, flew a circuit of the airfield and positioned the aircraft to come in and land. However, as he came into land, the aircraft suddenly nose-dived into the ground. Second Lieutenant Marks was killed instantly.

The inquest, which was held just a few hours after the accident reveals more detail: Lieutenant Fred Bradfield identified the body and said that the deceased was still training for his pilot's certificate. Captain Ronald Blatherwick of the Royal Flying Corps said he had been instructing the deceased since he had been at the aerodrome. He had only three and a half hours flying time and was on his first solo flight at between 7:45 pm and 8 pm. The witness sent him up on his first flight. He got off very well and made one complete circle and turned to come into the aerodrome. He turned alright and was gliding down when the machine suddenly nose-dived.

Captain Blatherwick was asked several searching questions at the inquest: The Coroner: "Was the machine in good order and the weather alright?" Captain Blatherwick: *"Yes I had been flying it myself and the weather was alright"* The Foreman of the jury: "Three and a half hours seems rather a short time to send a man up by himself." Captain Blatherwick: *"No three and a half is quite a lot to give a pupil. The average is 2 and a half to 3 hours"* A Juror: "Could you tell us what caused the accident?" Captain Blatherwick: *"My own private opinion is he pushed the nose down to glide into the aerodrome and pushed it too far and got into such a position that he could not get it out."* A Juror: "Do you think an experienced pilot would have been able to recover?" Captain Blatherwick: *"Well an experienced pilot would probably have never got into that position."*

Witness, Second Lieutenant James Cumin RFC described the fatal flight: *"The deceased got off very well from the ground and made one complete circuit of the aerodrome. There was a Southeast wind blowing and as the deceased got to the Northwest corner of the aerodrome he turned and glided a very short distance and suddenly nose-dived and came down."* The Coroner asked him "Can you account for the machine doing what it did?" Second Lieutenant James Cumin: *"Not unless he pushed the control too far forward, causing the machine to go straight down."*

A Farman MF 11 Shorthorn - not the crash involving Second Lieutenant Marks, but accidents were many on training squadron establishments.

Major Theodore Rodwell, the deceased's Commanding Officer stated in evidence that *"The machine was all right and the best possible machine for learners."* and Captain Willoughby Smith, Royal Army Medical Corps told the inquest *"The deceased's skull was fractured and several bones in his body were broken. Evidently some heavy body had fallen on his head and caused instantaneous death."*

The Coroner remarked that the occurrence was an unfortunate one, but these pupils had to learn to fly, and had to take risk in doing so. A verdict of accidental death was returned.

The verdict of accidental death was soon to come into question following a spate of further accidents at Waddington, the first occurring the very next day. A rumour began to circulate that there was a saboteur on the base and it was their nefarious activities that were the true cause.

An investigation was instigated which found that the accident rate was no greater than any other training base. What nobody at Waddington knew at the time was that the Shorthorn had an aerodynamic problem. Unlike modern aircraft, the tail plane provided a significant amount of lift and that lift could lead the aircraft to enter a much steeper descent than the pilot intended. To make matters worse the unintended dive would be very difficult to recover from, a situation very similar to that described in 2nd Lieutenant Marks accident.

The funeral took place on Saturday 5th May 1917 and was reported as

On the left Second Lieutenant Mark's gravestone as photographed some years ago, wrongly showing the RAF crest as the RAF was created on 1st April 1918 whereas on the right a more recently replaced stone shows the correct RFC crest

follows in the Lincolnshire Echo: '*The funeral of Second Lieutenant C Royston Marks who met his death on 3rd May took place here. The Royal Flying Corps who were in attendance fired the usual three volleys over the grave and two of the buglers sounded the Last Post. Lieutenant Johnson represented the parents. There were some very beautiful wreaths, including one from his mother and another from his comrades, which was in the form of an RFC wing*'.

Private John William Clarkson

North Staffordshire Regiment

Died 26th January 1918

By January 1918, the horrors of World War One were reaching their conclusion, but few could have imagined that the world was about to face a much deadlier foe. The Spanish Flu, or as it is now known, the H1N1 influenza virus, killed somewhere between 50 and 130 million people in an outbreak lasting from January 1918 until December 1920.

The name Spanish Flu is misleading; the disease was first detected in Kansas, North America, before reaching England and France. It was only later that it reached Spain, but because Spain was not involved in the war it was the first country the virus reached in which press censorship was not in force. Worried that the news of a deadly outbreak of disease would damage morale, the allied countries suppressed the news and it was thus that Spain was where the virus became known to the public.

The Spanish Flu had two unusual characteristics. Firstly it had a very high mortality rate with 20% of those infected succumbing. Secondly, it seemed to be particularly potent against young, fit adults. This was due to the way that the virus caused an overreaction by the body's immune system to such an extent that the body would attack itself.

In January 1918, Private John Clarkson was serving with the Labour Corps at the Musketry Camp in Ponteland, Northumberland. Before the war, he had lived at Rose Cottage in Waddington Village where he had worked as a Postman.

Today, the Labour Corps is known as the Royal Logistics Corps and during World War One they were responsible for providing logistical support to the fighting army. Most members of the Labour Corps were made up from those who could not achieve the A1 medical standard required to fight on the frontline; often this was because they had been wounded with their previous regiment and transferred.

Members of the Labour Corps often felt like second class citizens within the wider army, especially as those who died were buried under the auspices of their original regiment and it is for this reason that John Clarkson is recorded by the Imperial War Graves Commission as being a member of the North Staffordshire Regiment.

John Clarkson was born in Kensington, Middlesex, but his parents died whilst he was still young. Census records seem to indicate that he moved to Lincolnshire to live with his extended family at this point. History does not record whether John was a definite victim of the Spanish Flu, but he contracted the disease at the start of the outbreak and it would seem likely. His death certificate gives some indication of his suffering, stating that he died from Influenza 22 days, Exhaustion 20 days and heart failure 30 hours. This would be consistent with the way in which Spanish Flu would take an otherwise healthy young man.

When researching this book, no trace of John's grave could be found. In 2015 however, Andrew Ellison advised us as follows: 'Since retiring from the RAF in 2012 I have spent many hours in St Michael's Churchyard as a volunteer

gardener trying to restore it to the condition it was 20 years ago. In doing so I have removed much of the ivy, cut back shrubs and felled trees. This work has unearthed plaques, graves and many other interesting historical features and the names of local residents that were previously thought lost through the bombing or just forgotten. One such grave that has come to light is that of Pte J W Clarkson and following the work previously mentioned, the headstone is now clearly visible.(as can seen opposite) The headstone is not a CWGC stone, but possibly a family or Regimentally purchased memorial. Looking at the stone in detail I suspect it was placed in position after the church was bombed in WW2'.

Pilot Officer A N MacFarlane

Died 29th January 1938

In 1934 Lord Rothermere, owner of the Daily Mail, was sufficiently concerned about the Germans' apparent superiority in the air that he issued a challenge to the British aviation industry. The challenge was to produce a high-speed aircraft capable of carrying six passengers and two crew. The winner was Britain First, an aircraft that would soon become the Bristol Blenheim. Although superior in every way to the RAF's fighter bombers of the time, it would still prove woefully inadequate when it was later pitted against the cutting-edge technology of the Luftwaffe just a few years later.

Delivery of the new type to the RAF began in March 1937 and 44 Squadron at RAF Waddington received their bomber variants in June of that year. Their previous aircraft was a two seat biplane which owed more to the First World War than any future conflict, so the move from Hawker Hind to Bristol Blenheim must have been a welcome one.

A little over six months since the aircraft's introduction to squadron service, Pilot Officer MacFarlane was flying a solo training sortie over Lincolnshire. Just before 16:30hrs, he decided to perform a loop. Whether he flew the manoeuvre incorrectly or the stresses were just too great for the aircraft will never be known, but at some point, the whole tail empennage broke off. Knowing that the aircraft was doomed, Pilot Officer MacFarlane abandoned the aircraft and took to his parachute. Were it not for a cruel twist of fate, this is where the story should have ended. Unfortunately during the abandonment he suffered serious head injuries from which he died in hospital two days later. The aircraft crashed at Tattershall Thorpe near Coningsby

Samuel Palmer, a witness to the accident, said he saw the plane loop two or three times before the crash. Charles Danby from Coningsby, heard a crash and saw a man in a parachute pass over him. Having run over to where he landed, he found him lying on his back, choking for breath. At the inquest, Squadron Leader Tindall, of 44 Squadron, told the Coroner that MacFarlane had been detailed to conduct take-offs and landings, as well as practice flying on one engine, in a flight scheduled to last 1 hour 20 minutes. He also added what was perhaps the most crucial evidence: *"The plane MacFarlane was flying was not one that should have been put through the manoeuvers described by Palmer, it was too heavy. If the plane was looped in a heavy manner and at high speed, there would be a danger of the structure breaking"*.

Also at the inquest, Captain Frank Wilkins of the Accident Investigations Department of the Air Ministry stated he was convinced that parts of the plane which fell from it as it came down were broken as the result of impact by the pilot's body. If the pilot released the parachute a little too early he might have been swept through the tail of the plane and that would account for his injuries.

The wreckage of Pilot Officer MacFarlane's aircraft. Looking on is Flying Officer McKenzie RCAF

Pilot Officer MacFarlane was from New Zealand, serving on a Short Service Commission, having been trained to fly at number 8 Flying Training School at Filton near Bristol. Before the accident, he had amassed 256 hours flying, but only 7 of those had been on the Blenheim. Records show that an estate of £87 14s 8d went to William MacFarlane.

Aircraftman Norman Vincent Newsham

Died 20th March 1939

Monday the 20th March was a typical British Spring day, overcast with low cloud but otherwise unremarkable. The people of Boultham were going about their everyday business oblivious to the drama that was about to unfold quite literally in their backyards. At mid-day an aircraft thundered out of the gloom at full throttle in a vertical dive, only moments later crashing close to Boultham Baths in Lincoln.

Two Hampdens (L4171 and L4087) parked on the grass outside of Waddington's Watch Office around the same time.

Hampden L4082 of Waddington's 50 Squadron was returning from Eveden in Scotland when it crashed in an area of open ground between the baths and the Old Waterworks Cottages which were less than 30 yards from the crash site.

Mrs Martin who lived in the cottages was assisting with wash-day and later told of her experience: *"I scarcely had time to turn around after hearing the roar of the falling plane and the explosion as it hit the ground before flying pieces of the engine debris struck the wash-house and set fire to a pile of clothes that was beside the door. A big piece of metal struck the brickwork above the door lintel and pushed it out of line. The bits that came through the door were much smaller but they were blazing as they fell and they set fire to the clothes."*

Mrs Coxon, also of the Old Waterworks Cottages, was in the kitchen preparing a pudding for her family: *"There was a deafening explosion which shook the very foundations of the house and practically every picture fell from the walls. As I was rushing out to find what had happened there was a piece of blazing wreckage on the kitchen floor. I picked this up with my hands as I was afraid of it setting fire to the house and I threw it into the garden. I then saw half of a propeller between two and three feet in length on the lawn where the grass was smouldering. There were dense clouds of smoke coming from the plane."*

At the inquest, further witnesses came forward, but their testimony proved inconclusive. Witnesses differed in their versions of events, but some recalled the aircraft coming down in flames. It is very common for those witnessing an air crash to remember seeing the aircraft on fire or suffering from engine problems before it crashed. What is in fact happening is that, having seen a traumatic event, the brain fills in the blanks on a subconscious level. The brain sees a crash and assumes that there must have been a cause and fills that gap with what it sees as a logical assumption.

Today, video evidence often contradicts eye-witness accounts and has led to a much more cautious approach to this type of testimony.

PC Hammond who was perhaps more used to giving an objective version of what he witnessed told the inquest: *"I was on duty in High Street near South Bar-Square when the accident happened. I saw the machine at a height of between 500 and 600 feet. The pilot was evidently having trouble with one engine. The plane turned to the right and then dived with a terrific roar. For a moment it flattened out and a ring of black smoke followed by a cloud of black smoke came from it. I did not see any flames before it crashed."*

PC Hammond rushed to the accident site, but the aircraft's occupants were beyond any help. The aircraft had struck the ground with such violence that it took several hours of digging to reach the bodies. At the inquest, it was revealed that those who died could only be identified by fragments of their clothing. Newsham was only identified by his service number, which had been sewn into his sock.

The accident could have been much worse, the aircraft had missed the Jackson & Co Laundry by less than 100 yards. Not only were over 200 young women working inside, but the laundry contained a great deal of highly explosive chemicals.

Returning a verdict of Death by Misadventure, the Coroner, Dr G Wells-Cole, summed up as follows: *"It is very unlikely that the real cause of the accident would ever be discovered. There is no doubt at all that it was a pure accident. There is quite clearly no shadow of blame to be attached to the Royal Air Force or to anyone and we can only be thankful that the accident did not happen over a populated part of the city."*

What the Coroner did not know was that the RAF had already become concerned about the number of Hampden crashes. Even though the Hampden was still a relatively new aircraft an alarming number of accidents had the same symptoms. The aircraft would be flying along normally when it would suddenly dive into the ground for no reason. More often than not the aircraft had been in formation with other aircraft.

The RAF ordered the Central Flying School to investigate with Squadron Leader Stainthorpe (whose death in February 1941 features in our first book - Slightly Below the Glidepath 1 - RAF Scampton) leading the investigation.

He discovered two major issues, both concerning the very small rudders on the Hampden. Firstly, should an engine failure occur, the pilot was required to use excessive force on the rudder pedals in order to get sufficient effect from the rudders. A pilot of small stature might not have sufficient strength for this.

The second problem was that the rudders could suffer an aerodynamic condition called stabalised yaw. In certain conditions, the rudders could be susceptible to a side stream airflow blanking the tail control services. In particular, the loss of elevator control may have lead to a sudden and uncontrollable dive.

Also killed in the crash were Pilot Officer Robert McAlister of Glasgow, Sergeant Walter Freestone of Liverpool and Aircraftman Frederick Greensill of Middlewich in Cheshire.

Hampden L4082 seen at Waddington before the fatal flight

Flying Officer David Ivan Jobson
Sergeant J A Hawes
Sergeant E W Jones

Died 18th July 1939

In less than two months, World War Two would begin, but the RAF had been on a war-footing for some time. Despite having left it very late, the RAF was in a period of expansion and was training for the inevitability of war with Germany. With this in mind, twelve Hampdens of Waddington's 44 Squadron set off on a long range navigation exercise to France via RAF Tangmere in Sussex.

The weather was not good and low cloud combined with poor visibility would make it a very testing exercise. Not long into the flight, L4046 piloted by Flying officer Jobson got into difficulty. Whilst the formation began a climb into cloud, he seems to have been unable to maintain his position and broke away from the other aircraft. Shortly afterwards, having apparently lost control, the aircraft dived into the ground near Corby in Lincolnshire, killing all four occupants.

Mr F Bish, witnessed the crash from the ground. He stated that the aircraft had flown over once appearing lost and then flew over again when one aircraft dived steeply into the ground and crashed on the edge of a wood. Whilst there is no doubt that Mr Bish witnessed the crash, care must be taken with his interpretation of events. There is no way he could have known whether the aircraft was lost and it seems likely that the first aircraft he saw was a different

44 Squadron Hampdens at Waddington taken just before the outbreak of war

formation. However, his description of the aftermath does seem accurate. According to him, wreckage and human remains were spread over three fields. It is also consistent with reports that the explosion shook villages two miles away.

Three of the four crew lie buried at Waddington. The fourth member, Aircraftman Second Class R J Andrews, the aircraft's Wireless Operator, was returned home for burial.

Although Flying Officer Jobson was buried with his comrades, an unusual feature is that he has a private headstone. At the time, graves would have been marked with a simple wooden cross and it is possible that his family wanted to ensure he had a more permanent memorial. Secondly the accident occurred just before the start of the Second World War and there may have been uncertainty about the official headstone which for the other two crew either side of Jobson can be seen is not a standard Imperial War Graves Commission type.

Flying Officer Jobson's private headstone flanked by his two colleagues. Sergeant Hawes on the right and Sergeant Jones on the left. No detail of his rank or service connection is mentioned on Flying Officer Jobson's headstone..

Aircraftman Second Class Leonard James Penteny

Died 31st October 1939

Sergeant Cordle, the pilot of Hampden L4096, was relatively new to 50 Squadron. Having gained his wings at Filton on 16th September 1938 he had since amassed a total of 24 hours on Hampdens. Crucially, he had not flown at night since completing his training over a year before and this was to be his first night flight in a Hampden.

The weather was reasonable for an experienced pilot, but there was no moon and with the recent declaration of war, black-out conditions made it very dark indeed. The aircraft took-off normally and reached a height of about 1000 feet, it then dived steeply into the ground, crashing near Branston.

The investigation was damning, not only was an inexperienced pilot sent up in totally unsuitable conditions, it was also found that he was carrying an unauthorised passenger. On a pilot's first flight of any type it was normal practice to send minimal crew with him. Although it's impossible to say which of the two wireless operators the unauthorised passenger was, it is clear only one of them needed to be there.

The Chief of Air Staff was sufficiently annoyed to make the following comment on the accident report: '*Flight Commander and Squadron Commander to blame, poor. Pilot should not have been sent up in such conditions especially with a passenger. Letters of dissatisfaction to both officers.*'

It does seem that some lessons were learned as further comment was made that inexperienced pilots would be sent to reserve squadrons for more night flying. Also killed in the accident were Sergeant R S W Cordle and Aircraftman Burge a Wireless Operator.

Corporal Archibald McDonald Henderson

Died 23rd November 1939

World War Two was barely three months old when Corporal Henderson was killed at Waddington airfield. His death was due to a tragic set of circumstances involving a 49 Squadron Hampden aircraft from nearby RAF Scampton flown by Squadron Leader McGregor Watt. This accident also features in our book Slightly Below the Glide Path 1 – RAF Scampton, but the content is reproduced here to give the full circumstances.

The 23rd November 1939 was a typical November day, cold and foggy, with visibility down to just fifty yards. The weather was so bad that at first the 49 Squadron Commanding Officer had considered cancelling what was to become the fatal flight, but upon hearing that the pilot was Squadron Leader McGregor-Watt he was reassured and allowed it to go ahead. The squadron commander had good reason to be confident in his pilot. Squadron Leader McGregor-Watt was very experienced having been trained at the prestigious Royal Air Force College at Cranwell. He had been a pilot for just under thirteen years and had in that time amassed over 3000 hours flying.

For Squadron Leader McGregor-Watt, today's duty was to take Hampden L4034 from Scampton to Waddington where his three trainee wireless operators could practice ZZ landings under the guidance of their instructor Corporal Keating. Due to the local nature of the flight, it was not considered necessary to have a second pilot or navigator onboard.

L4034 when it first arrived at RAF Scampton as the first Hampden assigned to 49 Squadron.

ZZ was a blind approach system designed to allow an aircraft to land in bad weather, the initials standing for Zero visibility and Zero Cloud-base. In the days before radar it was a rudimentary, but essential means of landing the aircraft in poor visibility. The wireless operator would receive several radio bearings transmitted from the control tower on the airfield. These bearings would allow the pilot to work out his position relative to the airfield and line-up for a landing.

At around noon disaster struck. Having apparently misjudged the approach the twin engine Hampden roared across the airfield with its engines at full power and flying at only ten feet above the ground. In a desperate bid to avoid the control tower, which had appeared in front of him, the pilot put the aircraft into a steep bank to the right.

Despite narrowly missing the control tower the pilot was unable to avoid one of the airfield hangars and crashed onto its roof. The aircraft skipped across

LAC Walter Gerald Kelly

the roof before plunging to the ground. All those on board the aircraft were killed on impact or died shortly afterwards.

Sadly this accident also caused casualties on the ground. Three airmen of Waddington's 50 Squadron, including Corporal Henderson, who had been working in number two hangar, were killed when one of the engines from the aircraft fell through the roof onto their work area.

Investigations into the accident established that the radio aerial which transmitted the bearings to the pilot, was poorly sighted and this directly led to the crash. As a consequence the transmitter was re-sited and procedures improved to prevent future accidents.

The aircraft involved had been the first Hampden to be delivered to Bomber Command on 20th September 1938, making it just over one year old at the time of the crash.

Squadron Leader McGregor-Watt is buried in Nettleham New Churchyard just a few miles from Scampton whilst three of his crew, Corporal Thomas Alexander Keating, Leading Aircraftman Walter Gerald Kelly and Aircraftman First Class Stanley Taylor, the last two being trainee wireless operators, are buried in the military plot at Scampton Village Churchyard.

While Corporal Keating who was from Winchester was relatively old at 46, those killed in the hangar were much younger. Corporal Henderson was 24 and a native of Gosforth, Newcastle upon Tyne. Aircraftman First Class Leslie McGarvie (26) is buried in St Mary's Churchyard, Prestwich whilst Aircraftman Second Class Frank Talbot, who was only 18 years old is buried in Blackburn Cemetery.

Pilot Officer Kenneth Andre Cockerell

Died 19th June 1940

The 19th of June 1940 marked the day that the German General, Erwin Rommel occupied the French port of Cherbourg and Marshall Petain prepared for the surrender of France.

It was also the first day on which German bombers were seen in British skies and on the previous day, Winston Churchill had delivered the following speech: *"Hitler knows he will have to break us in this island or lose the war. If we can stand up to him, all Europe may be free and the life of the world may move forward into broad, sunlit uplands. But if we fail then the whole world, including the United States, including all that we have known and cared for, will sink into the abyss of a new dark age made more sinister, and perhaps more protracted, by the lights of perverted science. Let us therefore brace ourselves to our duties and so bear ourselves that if the British Empire and its Commonwealth last for a thousand years, men will say, This was their finest hour"*.

It was against this background of looming catastrophe that Kenneth Cockerell must have decided to have a day out with friends, and who could blame him. For a young airman at this stage of the war the future must have looked bleak and the prospect of a long and happy life remote.

Kenneth met his death in a road accident on the Lincoln to Sleaford Road at Temple Bruer, when he collided head-on with another car. He had been a member of 50 Squadron at RAF Waddington. Born in 1919 to his parents Harry and Madeleine in Teddington, Middlesex he only lived to the age of 21. Also killed in the crash, were his friends, Pilot Officer Alan Lawton (20) and Aircrafwoman First Class Barbara Williams (17) who was a member of the Women's Auxiliary Air Force. She died the following day in hospital.

Sergeant Edward Deryck Farmer

Died 1st August 1940

As a medium bomber, the Hampden was often operating at the limit of its endurance when striking targets on the continent. Missions lasting over 10 hours were not uncommon, but an aircraft would be on the very last of its fuel when it returned home. Even on more routine missions, there was not a lot of room for error as far as fuel was concerned and the smallest navigational mistake could prove catastrophic.

Hampden L4085 of 44 squadron had been on a mine-laying mission off the German coast. These missions were known as gardening missions and the mines were known as vegetables, the type of vegetable indicated the area in which the mine was to be dropped. It also involved locating a known point on the enemy coast and flying a timed leg at low speed to ensure that the mine was dropped precisely in the enemy sea lanes.

Having successfully dropped their mine, Sergeant Farmer, the pilot, set course for England. Unfortunately, the weather had deteriorated and they were unable to locate their position as they crossed the North Sea. It was only when they spotted the Irish coast that they realised that they had over-shot Waddington by quite some margin.

Realising the mistake, Sergeant Farmer turned his aircraft around and headed for home, but it was too late. At 6:30am they finally ran out of fuel and the engines stopped, the crew had enough time to put out an SOS on the radio before ditching in Cardigan Bay.

Naval Petty Officer supervises the arming of an anti ship mine prior to a Gardening Mission

All Hampdens carried a life raft in the upper surface of the port wing and this would be automatically deployed if it came into contact with salt water. Sure enough, the life raft deployed, but due to a split, it completely failed to inflate. Even though it was August the crew's chances of survival without a life raft were severely diminished.

The Aberystwyth lifeboat Frederick Angus was launched at 7:26am and despite being joined in the search by the motor boat Emerald Star, only two of the crew could be saved. Sergeants Hobbs and Seager required hospital treatment, but made a full recovery. Sergeants Farmer and Wood were not so lucky and died of exposure before they were found. For Sergeant Seager, his bad luck was not yet over. Returning to Waddington from his survivor's leave, he was hit by an anti-aircraft shell whilst waiting at a station for his train and lost a leg.

In December 2009, Jason Hicks and his boat crew were fishing for scallops off the Welsh Coast, when the propeller assembly of L4085 became entangled in their nets. This sad reminder of the crash is now on display at Greendale Farm Shop, Sidmouth Road, Exeter.

Interestingly, Sergeant Farmer was a native of Lincoln, the son of Edward and Edith Mary Farmer. Sergeant Cyril Edward Thomas Wood was sent home to Oxford for burial.

A 44 Squadron Hampden (L4088) which was lost during a mine laying sortie from Waddington on 22nd April 1940. A very similar mission to the one carried out by Sergeant Farmer and his crew. The crew of L4088 were shot down but survived and became the first complete Hampden crew (4 of them) to be taken as Prisoners of War.

Pilot Officer Jack Milton Cave

Died 30th October 1940

Pilot Officer Cave was the pilot of a 101 Squadron Blenheim from RAF West Raynham. His squadron had been ordered to take-off before dusk due to a belt of rain which was expected to reach their base around midnight. Returning from his target in Germany, it was 23:00 hours when he was over the skies of Waddington. It is not known what went wrong but the aircraft crashed into a wood near the village of Coleby, just south of the base.

Jack was a New Zealander from Whakatane, Auckland and as such a home burial was not an option for him. In accordance with normal procedures at the time the RAF station closest to the crash site was responsible for his burial and hence the reason he is buried in Waddington.

Jack's brother Vernon was also a member of the Royal New Zealand Air Force and he too was sadly to die in Serbia in 1945.

Flying Officer Hugh Vernon Matthews DFC
Sergeant Henry Cecil Redgrave
Sergeant Roy Desmond Welch

Died 13th March 1941

The Avro Manchester was to gain a reputation as a dreadful aircraft, its two Rolls Royce Vulture engines proving both under powered and unreliable. However, in early 1941, 207 Squadron at Waddington were still doing their best to make their recently acquired aircraft operationally effective.

On the night of 13th March 1941, 207 Squadron had been ordered to provide two aircraft as part of a total force of 139 attacking the Blohm & Voss shipyard in Hamburg. In the event, obviously keen to demonstrate the potential of their new aircraft, they managed to provide five.

The first four aircraft took-off without incident, but Hugh Matthews' aircraft was running late after the tail wheel had burst. Although only a short delay, enough time had elapsed since the flare path had been lit to attract the attention of a German night fighter pilot.

Hugh Matthews DFC

Leutnant Hans Hahn of Nachtjagdgeschwader 2 based at Gilze-Rijen in Holland was prowling the night skies of Lincolnshire in his Junkers 88 waiting for just such an opportunity.

As Hugh Matthews accelerated his aircraft down the runway, Hans Hahn made his attack, devastating the Manchester with his Junkers 88's cannon fire. On fire and mortally wounded, the Manchester staggered into the air, only to crash at Whisby on the outskirts of Lincoln a few minutes later.

All but two of the crew died immediately. Sergeants Cox and Martin were thrown clear, but Sergeant Martin was to die later of his injuries in Lincoln Hospital. Despite losing one of his legs Sergeant Cox became the only member of the crew to survive. Although only a few moments into the flight, L7313 earned the dubious distinction of becoming the first Manchester to be lost on operations.

Also killed were Sergeant Joseph Marsden who was buried in Bolton and Sergeant Harry Hemingway who was buried in Dunston.

A Waddington Manchester of 207 Squadron

Hans Hahn

Leutnant Hans Hahn was to achieve 12 victories over the skies of Lincolnshire, earning both the Knights Cross and Iron Cross. On one occasion he even attacked a Beaufighter, piloted by Guy Gibson at RAF Wellingore and came very close to changing the course of history. Following several close shaves where his aircraft had been damaged in combat, he met his end in his familiar hunting ground. Less than seven months later on 11th of October 1941, he misjudged his attack on an Airspeed Oxford over Grantham and collided with it. There were no survivors from either aircraft.

An Oxford aircraft - this one was used by Beam Approach Training (BAT) Flights

Sergeant Phillip Charles Livesey Wicks
Sergeant William Edgar Godfrey

Died 3rd April 1941

The German Battleships Scharnhorst and Gneisenau were a potent force in the North Atlantic. In January 1941 the two ships sailed and began Operation Berlin, the aim of their mission was to destroy the convoy ships that were the lifeblood of Britain's war effort. By March the pair had sunk nine ships, but the intervention of HMS Rodney and HMS King George V caused the task force

force commander, Admiral Lutjens to run for port. In truth, this was a tactically sound plan, he was outgunned by the Royal Navy and in any case his ship needed urgent repairs to the boiler. On 22ⁿᵈ March the two ships entered port at Brest and began their repairs.

The opportunity to destroy two of Germany's most valuable ships whilst vulnerable in port did not go unnoticed by the RAF and by 3ʳᵈ of April they had attempted at least six bombing raids. Every time cloud cover had prevented any effective attack. On the night of 3/4ᵗʰ April a force of ninety aircraft was once again tasked against the German battleships and whilst most of the force did bomb, they reported that the target was difficult to locate. Unsurprisingly, no damage was caused to the ships.

At 19:04 hours, 24 year old Sergeant Kenneth George William Kyle, the pilot of Whitley P4947, took-off from RAF Topcliffe in North Yorkshire as part of this mission. The weather was cloudy with rain and drizzle, but certainly within the safe operating limits of the aircraft.

Three and a half hours later, they were back over England and in trouble. For whatever reason, they had not found their target and so still had their bombs on board, but more worryingly the aircraft was icing up.

The pilot must have decided that he needed to land sooner rather than later and elected to make an approach to RAF Waddington. Being unfamiliar with Waddington, he seems to have misjudged his landing and applied full power to go around for another try. The combination of the extra weight from the bomb load and the damaging effect of ice on the aircraft's performance were too much for Sergeant Kyle and the aircraft stalled at 300 feet and crashed.

A Whitley bomber

As well as those buried at Waddington, Sergeant Kenneth George Kyle and Flight Sergeant Alan Leigh Kennedy were also killed. They were returned home for burial and are buried respectively in Wellingborough and Manchester. Miraculously, although severely injured one of the crew, Sergeant Engels survived.

The bombing of Waddington Village
9th May 1941

Although not directly featuring people who are buried in St Michael's Churchyard, the story of the bombing of Waddington village in 1941 lies well in this book. It clearly shows the dangers of living so close to one of the main bomber bases in Lincolnshire and the threat to the civilians and support services of the station, as well as the military personnel.

In the early hours of 9th May 1941, the German Luftwaffe attacked Waddington Aerodrome and released two parachute mines overhead the airfield. As the mines dropped towards the ground their parachutes were caught by the wind, drifting them clear of the airfield and landing on the village. The first mine struck St Michael's Church destroying it completely.

The second fell in the Vicarage garden making a huge crater. As well as destroying the church and quite a large area of its churchyard the two mines destroyed 19 houses, badly damaged a further 71 with another 160 slightly damaged.

A total of 400 villagers were left homeless until repairs were carried out. One person was killed, six received serious injuries and forty three suffered slight injuries.

The person who died was twenty year old Eva Gibson Hall. She was in service at the Rectory. That night she

The original beautiful church in Waddington Village

46

What remained of the church the morning after

had been to a dance and decided to stay at her grandmothers in Bar Lane, adjacent to the church. She was seriously injured as a huge piece of masonry crashed through onto her bed as she slept. She was rescued, but died later that day in hospital. Interestingly, had she slept in her normal bed in the rectory she would still have perished as the chimney of the rectory crashed through the roof and

An iconic picture of the church bells in the rubble

landed on her bed. It is also believed that two elderly residents later died of heart attacks.

The damage to such a small village was extensive. The local community had received many air raid warnings, but actual attacks were limited. This one was the exception. However the two land mines were not the end of the German attack that night.

Within a couple of hours a lone attacker dropped a stick of bombs onto the airfield and its various buildings. The first exploded in a field behind the Sergeants' Mess, a second on the road leading to it. The third struck an air raid shelter, the fourth struck the building housing the NAAFI and the fifth fell on the parade ground

The staff, who had vacated the NAAFI building, presumably on hearing the air raid siren and   station personnel, had taken to the nearby trench shelter when the bomb landed on it, causing the death of seven NAAFI ladies and newly arrived 44 Squadron pilot Sergeant Joseph Raymond Vigar (21). He is buried

RAF photographs of the damage to the building which held the NAAFI. It was quickly rebuilt and renamed the "Raven Club" in honour of Doris Raven, the NAAFI Manageress who died in the bombing along with several other ladies.

in Smallfield, Surrey. Some accounts put the death toll at eleven, including three members from the Women's Auxiliary Air Force (WAAF), but extensive research has failed to establish any WAAFs being killed.

The new St Michael's Church

The seven members of the NAAFI staff who died were, manageress, Doris Raven (42, Joan Bodinner (28), Elizabeth Turner (16), Alice Brown (31) Minnie Easton (26) and Frances Nacey (20) and Reneie May Woods (23).

One girl, Lily Green, was pulled out alive. The names of all the civilians who died that night are commemorated in the Civilian War Dead Roll of Honour located near St George's Chapel in Westminster Abbey. It contains 67,092 names of the civilan war dead.

The NAAFI building was soon rebuilt and renamed the Raven Club in honour of Doris Raven, the NAAFI Manageress on this fateful night. It is still named after her to this day.

Sergeant William Robert Bain Relyea RCAF

Died 22nd July 1941

It is a little known fact that as many people in Bomber Command were killed in accidents as those who were killed as a result of enemy action. The reasons for such an appallingly high accident rate were largely the inexperience of the crews and the pressures of war having reduced training to the absolute minimum. Most of the time, these accidents occurred without civilian casualties, but this was not always the case.

Sergeant Relyea was an Observer on 44 Squadron Hampden AD983 whose mission was to drop anti-shipping mines around the Frisian Islands. His pilot, Sergeant Bruce had successfully returned to Lincolnshire after a five hour mission, but at 4am inexperience took its toll.

With only 93 hours flying experience, it is perhaps not surprising that the difficult conditions proved too much for Sgt Bruce. It was a particularly dark night which required a delicate balance of visual and instrument flying, but for reasons unknown Sergeant Bruce lost control of his aircraft.

The tail of the aircraft lies over the wall of Lincoln Girls' High School

All four crew were killed in the subsequent crash and to make matters worse it had crashed in the centre of Lincoln. The stricken Hampden had hit the Greestones staff residence attached to Lincoln Girls' High School on Lindum Road and immediately started a fierce fire. Despite two engines from the City Fire Brigade being quickly on the scene, the fire had taken hold and took two hours to extinguish.

Meanwhile five members of school staff were attempting to make their escape. Although four succeeded, one, Miss Fowler died. She had made it out of her own room and on to the windowsill of a second, but collapsed before making good her escape. Miss Fowler, the 49 year old French Mistress at Lincoln Girls' School, had been educated in Lausanne and moved to Lincoln from Gravesend in 1920. Miss L E Savill, the school's Headmistress said of her, *"She had been with us for 21 years and was a valued colleague and friend of the school. She will be greatly missed."*

As well as Sergeant Relyea, Sergeants Donald Macdonald Bruce, James Aloysius Connolly and Peter Joseph Lynch were also killed in the aircraft. Only Sergeant Relyea was buried at Waddington, his crew mates were all returned to their home towns for burial. Bruce is buried in the New Kilpatrick Cemetery in Dunbartonshire, Connolly, a fellow Scot, in Edinburgh Roman Catholic Cemetery and Lynch who hailed from the London area rests in the Streatham Park Cemetery.

William Relyea was a Canadian and member of the Royal Canadian Air Force. A Single man fromToronto he had joined up in July 1940. His recruiting officer described him as: Good type - pleasant, intelligent, good physique. Mature, frank and honest. Experienced - should absorb instructions easily. Steady nerves, anxious to fly. Strongly recommended.

Sergeant Gilbert Derrick Dodds RCAF
Sergeant Alan Forsythe
Sergeant Godfrey Michael Le Blanc Smith

Died 1st August 1941

Following any major maintenance, an aircraft would require an air test, the aim of the test was to ensure everything on the aircraft functioned correctly and that it was fit for operations. These flights were also seen as an opportunity to take some of the groundcrew who had worked on the aircraft flying. There is no doubt that flying in an aircraft you had just repaired is a great motivation to ensure you strived for perfection.

What went wrong with Hampden AD966 will never be known, but at 17:10 hours it crashed near South Park, Bracebridge Heath near Lincoln. Three aircrew and t2wo ground crew on board died.There was some speculation that the aircraft may have been damaged whilst low flying, but this was never confirmed.

The aircraft had lost its bomb bay doors before the crash, but investigators were unable to determine whether they were lost after striking an object in flight or whether they were ripped off by the unusual air load the aircraft was put under following the loss of control.

Buried at Waddington were Sergeant Le Blanc-Smith who was the aircraft's pilot, Sergeant Dodds the Observer and Sergeant Forsythe the Wireless Operator/Air Gunner. Others killed were the ground crew flying on that trip, Aircraftman First ClassThomas Bernard Jeffcote, an instrument repairer and Aircraftman First Class Arthur Douglas Clark, a pilot under training. Although classified as a pilot under training, as an Aircraftman First Class, it is likely that Clark was working at Waddington in another capacity until he got a place on a flying training course. Both Jeffcote and Clark were also buried in Lincolnshire, Clark in Crowle Cemetery, near Scunthorpe and Jeffcote in Lincoln (Newport) Cemetery.

Lincoln (Newport) Cemetery where Thomas Jeffcote lies buried

Sergeant Dodds was a Canadian fromToronto who joined the Royal Canadian Air Force in June 1940. He moved to the United Kingdom in May 1941 having married his wife June only a few months earlier. He was described by his recruiiting officer as very much interested and eager for a chance to be trained as a pilot. Good type and build, erect, clean cut, bright - good intellect, accustomed to work, courteous and pleasant. He did not go on to realise his dream of being a pilot and was the Observer on board the aircraft.

Sergeant William Joseph McQuade RCAF

Died 6th August 1941

Every Squadron in the RAF maintains an Operational Record Book and the entry dealing with Sergeant McQuade's death not only gives an insight into the operation that was undertaken and the weather in which it was conducted, but also the matter of fact way in which such losses were dealt with.

The 44 Squadron entry for 6th August 1941 reads as follows:

Weather. *Continuous slight rain for the first three hours, with light showers in evening. Low cloud-variable amounts rising from 1,300ft and remaining at 3,500ft, dispersing about 22.00 BST. Visibility not less than 5 miles. Wind moderate WNW'ly backing to light WSW'ly.*

Operations. *One Wellington of No.1 Group, three of No.3 Group with three Whitleys and eleven Hampdens were detailed to bomb docks and shipping at CALAIS, of this number seven Hampdens from this squadron were operating. Four of the Squadron's aircraft (Sgts De Brath, Dedman, Redfern and Musgrave) reached their objective and dropped their bombs in the docks area. The remaining three (Sgts Knight, Harvey and Nicholson) being unable to identify the target area returned to base with their bombs in accordance with "briefing" instructions that "bombs were to be dropped on the target only". An eighth Hampden No. X.2917 (Sgt Bradbury) crashed in a wood near Marham Satellite.*

The Marham Satellite mentioned above was RAF Barton Bendish and the aircraft had crashed there following a loss of control in adverse weather. The accident report noted that the pilot's instrument training had not taken place in the Hampden, but the Avro Anson instead. The Anson was a much more basic aircraft than the Hampden and was only used because the Hampden lacked dual controls. The clear implication was that Sergeant Bradbury's training had not been sufficient to fly the more complex aircraft on operations at night and in poor weather.

Sergeant McQuade was originally from Toronto in Canada and had been the Observer on the aircraft. This role later become known as navigator, a much more accurate description of the job. He joined the Royal Canadian Air Force in June 1940 and married Grace Sharpe on 25th January 1941.

Just two months later he moved to the United Kingdom and had been with 44 Squadron for only two months before he died. His recruiting officer wrote on his application form *'In my opinion applicant is exceptionally good material. Quiet and gentlemanly. Excellent.'*

The others who died were returned home for burial. They were Sergeant Gordon Stephenson Bradbury, Sergeant David Hinton Howe and Flight Sergeant Samuel David Yeomans, who despite being only 19 years old had already been awarded the Distinguished Flying Medal.

A typical Hampden crew at Waddington having returned from a mission

Aircraftman Second Class Frank Burdett Prest
Died 31st August 1941

In the crowded skies of wartime Lincolnshire even a routine mission held its dangers. As the 44 Squadron Hampden lined up for take-off at Waddington its pilot, Pilot Officer Owen could hardly have realised that moments later he and his entire crew would be dead. As Hampden AD939 climbed away from the airfield heading south it was struck by a Spitfire of 412 (Falcon) Squadron from nearby RAF Digby.

The pilot of the Spitfire (AD8586) was Pilot Officer William Robert Hughes of the Royal Canadian Air Force who had joined his squadron only five days earlier, fresh out of training. Prior to the accident he had been airborne for 45 minutes in weather that was later described as 'Rather hazy'. Following the collision both aircraft dived vertically into the ground killing all on board.

A photograph of a Spitfire formating - this one for fighter affiliation

The Officer Commanding 44 Squadron obviously felt that the blame lay with the Spitfire pilot, stating in the accident report that *'I attach no blame for this accident to the Hampden Captain. The Hampden was hit by a Spitfire shortly after the Hampden had taken off'.*

It must however be remembered that wartime training only gave pilots the minimum of experience before sending them to a frontline squadron. The Hampden pilot had only 27 hours experience of the type and the Spitfire's pilot had only been on his squadron for five days and had only been in the Royal Canadian Air Force for ten months. It is perhaps fairer to say that the accident was caused by inexperience brought about by the urgency of war.

Although four people were killed in total, only Frank Prest is buried at Waddington. He was 20 years of age and a prospective aircrew trainee, who on this day, was merely along for the ride. Pilot Officer Hughes (25) the Spitfire pilot, is buried in nearby Scopwick. Pilot Officer Patrick Owen, (21) the Hampden pilot, is buried in Lincoln Newport Cemetery and Flight Sergeant David Forbes (21) is buried in Peterhead.

Sergeant Archibald Allen Watt
Sergeant Eddy Stewart Cox

Died 7th September 1941

On this night, Bomber Command were attacking a wide range of targets. As well as sending a significant force to attack Berlin, they were also attacking the submarine yard in Kiel and the docks at Boulogne. Amongst this force, a small section of 8 Hampdens were tasked to lay anti-shipping mines off the Frisian Islands.

44 Squadron were to supply four suitably armed Hampdens to form part of the mine-laying force and at 21:15 the last of these aircraft took-off en-route to their target. For the crew of X2921 things started to go wrong almost immediately. As the station Commander was later to observe, the pilot failed to get the tail of the Hampden up, which produced too much drag for the aircraft to gain speed normally. Despite staggering into the air with the minimum of speed, the aircraft finally lost its battle for airspeed over Branston Hall Farm and crashed just two minutes later.

The combination of a full fuel load and the detonation of its mine caused the total destruction of the aircraft along with any evidence that might have helped the enquiry. All four crew were killed instantly. Sergeants Cox and Watt are buried in Waddington Churchyard whilst Sergeant Adrian Wimbush is buried in Birmingham and Sergeant James Newcombe in Dagenham.

Archibald Watt was originally from Salisbury, Rhodesia and a poignant reminder of him was to surface nearly 70 years later at the crash site.

In 2007 Mr Sid Deaton was searching the field where the crash occurred with his metal detector. Amongst the small metallic fragments he uncovered that remained in the field, was a watch bezel inscribed with the name of A.A. Watt and a 1939 coin (See below). Following an exhaustive, but ultimately unsuccessful search for family members, the watch is now on loan to the RAF Waddington Heritage Centre.

A Hampden aircrew and ground crew pose for a picture

Pilot Officer John Russell Clements
Flying Officer Ernest Edwin Gordon Crump
Aircraftman 2 James William Grace

Died 15th September 1941

When one of 207 Squadron's Manchester's suffered a technical fault at RAF Millom in Cumberland, the simplest answer was to fly a team of engineers over there to fix it. Having succeeded in their task and with the repaired aircraft having already landed ahead of them, the crew of Manchester L7318 together with the engineering party joined the Waddington circuit and prepared to land following their return flight.

Flying regulations stated that, on landing, the Bomb Aimer's compartment in the nose of the aircraft must be evacuated and it seems more than likely that those passengers who had been enjoying the view would have been asked to move to the rear of the aircraft, passing the pilot as they did so.

It was thought at the time that a number of people passing through a cramped cockpit and perhaps knocking the flap lever might go some way to explaining the tragic events that were about to unfold.

Squadron Leader Beauchamp, Officer Commanding B Flight, 207 Squadron takes up the story: *"At approximately 18:00 hours I was standing in front of the Officers' Mess awaiting the return of Manchester L7318 from Millom. I observed the aircraft do a normal circuit of the aerodrome at 800 feet when on its second circuit and approximately 3 miles west of the aerodrome the aircraft suddenly went into a dive of 70-80 degrees, and continued the dive without any apparent attempt to pull out. The aircraft struck the ground and burst into flames"*.

Mr E. Yeomans, a plumber from Church Road, South Hykeham also gives his account: *"At about 18:05 hours I had just got off the bus at Lawrence's Garage on the main Lincoln to Newark road and was walking home when I saw a Manchester aircraft flying over North Hykeham in the direction of South Hykeham at a height of about 500 feet. The engine sounded to be making a peculiar noise. As I watched the plane, the nose rose sharply and the plane appeared to climb for a few seconds. Immediately afterwards the nose dropped suddenly and the plane dived towards the ground. During the dive I could not hear the engines. The plane passed out of my view behind the trees still diving*

A 207 Squadron Manchester Bomber. This one was L7288

steeply. Almost immediately afterwards there was a loud explosion and smoke and flames shot up into the air. I was about half a mile distant from the plane when I first saw it. The weather was fine but dull".

The aircraft had crashed in fields at the bottom of Meadow Lane, a few hundred yards from St Michael's Church, killing all ten on board. Such was the violence of the crash that very little material evidence survived and much of the subsequent enquiry can only be seen as a well-founded theory of the cause. It was normal practice for the pilot of a Manchester to select twenty five degrees of flap and slow the aircraft in preparation for landing.

It would seem likely that having done this, one of the passengers accidentally knocked the flap lever back into the up position. At low speed and without the extra lift generated by the flaps, the aircraft would stall and fall out of the sky, in much the same way that the eye-witnesses had described.

Two days after the accident Flying Officer Herring of 207 Squadron was asked to put this theory to the test: *"I am a first pilot on Manchester aircraft in 207 Squadron. On the orders of the Commanding Officer I carried out the following test on 17th September 1941. I put the flaps down to 25 degrees and trimmed the aircraft to fly straight and level at an airspeed of 140 mph. I then*

knocked the flap lever back thereby taking the flap off. The result was that I went into quite a steep dive which I was unable to pull out of by means of the control column alone. I think it would be a dangerous manoeuvre low down".

Although it was impossible to conclusively prove that the accident was caused by the inadvertent knocking of the flap lever, procedures were put in place in order to try and prevent any such event in the future.

The picture opposite shows the inside of the cockpit and the route past the pilot from the Bomb Aimer's position.

A view looking from the back of a Manchester forward to the pilot's station

Those buried at Waddington are: Flying Officer Ernest Crump, the 25 year-old pilot who was from Leicester in South Africa, Pilot Officer John Clements, a Canadian from Milton, Ontario who had graduated from the University of Toronto as a Bachelor of Science and had previously worked as a mining engineer in the Hollinger Gold mine in Timmins, Ontario and James Grace (31), one of the engineers on board.

Others who died in the accident and were sent home for burial were: Pilot Officer John Patrick Anthony Sawyer (24) from Beaconsfield. His father Lieutenant R H Sawyer (RAF) had died on active service in 1918. Aircraftman 2 Jack Lister, a Lincoln man. Leading Aircraftman Leslie Wilfred Carter (24) another Lincoln man. Leading Aircraftman John Frederick Riding (18) of Stretford. Leading Aircraftman Harold Francis Winter (20) from Dewsbury and Aircraftman 1 Reginald Boyd (26) from Scunthorpe. Sergeant Norman Alan Mathison was another crew member killed that day. He is buried in Northallerton.

Reproduced below is the content of an interesting letter sent by Alan to his ex Head Teacher in April 1941 telling of his new life in the Royal Air Force.

1058529 Mathison. N.A.
Hut 54 W.
'A' Squadron. 4 Wing.
RAF. Wilts.
28th April 1941.

Dear Mr Palmer,
I received a copy of the school magazine which was addressed to me at home and I am grateful for it. Various parts bring back pleasant memories and I often think of my old school days and the good times I had.

Many of the things I was taught at school are now proving useful to me. Scouting and the experiences gained in camp life have also proved a wonderful help in my training. I am thoroughly enjoying myself and have had no dull moments. I experienced my first crash last week when a Polish instructor and myself went up in an unserviceable plane without realising it. We crashed on attempting to land. I was most fortunate and escaped with only a cut hand.

I am looking forward to 14 days leave which I have been promised. I am due to get it on or about May 9th. I am working exceptionally hard to make sure I do get it.
Kind regards to all.
Yours sincerely,
N. Alan Mathison.

Although the Manchester ultimately proved a failure, the aircraft was redeveloped with four Merlin engines and emerged as the legendary Lancaster, the most successful heavy bomber of World War Two.

A Lancaster bomber operating out of Waddington in 1944

Pilot Officer William Francis McCarthy RCAF
Pilot Officer William James Murray RCAF

Died 14th April 1942

Pilot Officer McCarthy

Having returned only the previous night from a successful mine laying operation, the crew of Hampden AT219 of 420 Squadron RCAF were tasked for operations against Dortmund. Shortly after take-off the pilot William Murray was faced with every pilot's worst nightmare, an engine failure at low-level. To make matters worse his aircraft was heavily laden with both fuel and a 2000 pound high-explosive bomb.

A cardinal rule of the time was to never turn the aircraft in the direction of a failed engine, due to the almost inevitable loss of control that would follow. In his haste to regain the safety of the airfield, William Murray broke this rule and at 21:45 hours his aircraft crashed at North Hykeham near Lincoln. Three of the crew died immediately and the fourth, Flight Sergeant Johnson, died in hospital the next day.

Before joining the Royal Canadian Air Force, the aircraft's Observer, William McCarthy had spent two years at the University of Toronto. It would seem that he had wanted to follow in his father's footsteps and become a lawyer.

William Murray, also from Canada, was from Medicine Hat, Alberta where his father, originally from Aberdeen, worked as a Fireman on the Canadian Pacific Railroad. After leaving school William had worked as an assistant chemist and as an apprentice printer.

Both of the Canadian crew were laid to rest at Waddington at 09:00hrs on 20th April 1942. Flight Sergeant Johnson, the Wireless Operator/Air Gunner was buried at Fordham and Sergeant Kenneth Birch, the other Air Gunner was buried in Yardley Wood.

Flight Sergeant Joseph Corbin Pritchard RCAF
Sergeant Herschel Homer Davis RCAF
Sergeant Gerald Grenville Joseph Laronde RCAF
Sergeant Geoffrey Albert Player

Died 20th April 1942

Inside a Hampden cockpit

Minutes into a routine cross country training flight, Sergeant Herschel Davis, the pilot of Hampden AD869 lost control of his aircraft and crashed at Wispington, three miles northwest of Horncastle. A court of inquiry later established that the aircraft had been allowed to take-off in an unserviceable condition and cited ground-crew negligence as the reason. All four crew members were killed instantly.

A particularly difficult case to research, visitors to these graves will note that different dates are used on each headstone. Laronde is shown as dying on the 21st and Player is shown as dying on the 19th whilst the remainder of the crew are recorded as the 20th. At first, it was thought that perhaps crew members had died in the days following the incident, but the accident record clearly shows that all died at the scene on the 20th.

The fact that the flight took-off at 00:30hrs on the 20th goes someway to explaining the confusion, but it was only a close examination of the individuals service record that revealed poor record keeping as the true cause.

In the case of Laronde, his Royal Canadian Air Force record of service has him recorded as dying on the 19th, 20th and 21st in different parts of the file, but in all cases he is recorded as dying at the scene, without being admitted to hospital.

The greatest weight of evidence indicates that they all died at the scene of the accident in the early hours of the morning of 20th April. It is perhaps indicative of how many accidents were occurring at the time, that those responsible for making the appropriate entries on the file rushed the job and in doing so, made mistakes.

Herschel Davis was an American, originally from Portland Oregon. Before Pearl Harbour, a common route for Americans who wanted to join the war effort was to cross the border into Canada and join the RCAF. Herschel had been brought up on the family farm and had been married at 20 to a teacher in Alaska. By the age of 24 he was divorced after the search for work had led to him and his wife ending up on opposite sides of the continent.

Gerald Laronde was from North Bay, Ontario and had joined the RCAF straight after leaving high school. Like many Canadians he enjoyed playing softball and hockey and before joining-up he had been learning his father's trade as a painter and paper-hanger. He was one of the crew's air gunners.

Joseph Pritchard was the Observer, but like many he had originally had ambitions of becoming a pilot. He was from Edmonton, Alberta and before joining the Royal Canadian Air Force he had been employed as a clerk for the Canadian National Telegraph. A keen basketball player, he also enjoyed playing the guitar and violin.

Geoffrey Player, the other Air Gunner, was the only British crew-member on board, and unfortunately due to the RAF having a different policy on the release of service records, nothing is known of his background.

Flight Sergeant Charles Arthur Parke RCAF

Died 25th April 1942

Following basic flying training, and before progressing to their operational squadrons, crews first had to pass through an Operational Training Unit (OTU). Here they would turn the basic skill of being able to fly an aeroplane into the ability to use it as a weapon of war. 11 OTU at RAF Steeple Morden used the Vickers Wellington to train prospective bomber crews.

At 04:11 hours on the morning of 25th April 1942, Wellington R1661 piloted by Sergeant Telford was making an approach to RAF Waddington. The weather at his home base was unsuitable, but at Waddington there was a bright moon with no cloud and at least twelve miles visibility.

Because it was still dark, the pilot was using the airfield's Drem lighting system to make his approach. Telford had never used the Drem system before, but had received a full briefing before the flight which included the use of a scale model as seen opposite.

The Drem Lighting system was invented by the RAF Drem Station Commander, Wing Commander Atcherly. The system was designed to allow pilots to land at night, without making the airfield an easy target for enemy bomber pilots. In order to do this, carefully shrouded lights shone a narrow beam of light that could only be seen once on the correct approach path.

Lights placed around the airfield guided the pilot onto the correct approach. The final two lights, known as totems, were on ten foot poles and indicated that the runway threshold was just ahead.

It appears that on this occasion the pilot's lack of familiarity with the system caused him to misjudge his approach.

The aerodrome control pilot witnessed the incident and gave the following statement: *"At approximately 04:10 hours I gave Wellington aircraft Whitworth E a Green Aldis lamp for permission to land. He acknowledged by switching on his downward recognition light. He then made a wide circuit preparatory to landing. I then observed he was approaching very low, so that when he was approximately 200 yards from me I gave him a Red Aldis Flash. Immediately after this he crashed into the sewage plant and caught fire".*

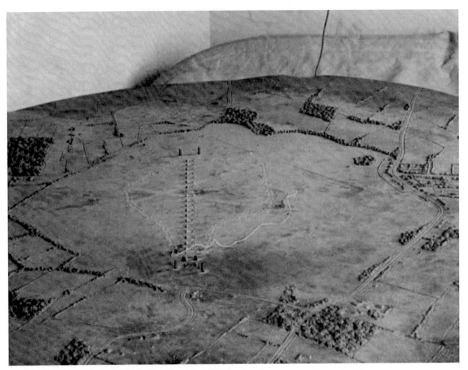

An example of the scale model used to demonstrate Drem Lighting

A copy of a photograph attached to Charles Parke's Canadian Service Record. He is on the right.

The crash site was about 500 yards short of the final totem lights, indicating that the approach had been very low indeed. Out of the crew of six there were two recorded survivors, Sergeants Marsden and Woodward. Both were taken to Bracebridge Heath Military Hospital and were off the medical list by 28th April. Records seem to indicate that they subsequently survived the war.

Charles Parke was originally from Caledonia, Ontario where he worked as a dairy farmer and stated his reason for leaving this occupation as "To help win the war." After arriving in England, he married a London girl,

Isobel Johnson of Earls Court. He was buried at Waddington at 11:00 hours on 29th April 1942.

Also killed that night were Pilot Officer Henry Snelling who is buried in Norwich and Sergeant Donald Telford, buried in Longbenton. Some records indicate that an unnamed Observer survived uninjured.

Flight Sergeant Roy Davidson RCAF

Died 21st June 1942

Flt Sergeant Davidson

Flight Sergeant Davidson was one of two air gunners in a Hampden attacking the German town of Emden. As was so often the case, the aircraft was hit by light flak as it returned to Waddington, injuring Davidson and Sergeant Murray. Despite his damaged aircraft, the pilot managed to get both crew members back to their home base where he knew they would get the best possible medical care.

At 05:03 hours on the 20th June, just after the aircraft landed, Davidson was admitted to the station medical centre where his injuries were described as follows: Fractures to the left lower leg and arm, abrasions and shrapnel wounds, shock and severe bleeding. Sadly, a little under 24 hours later at 02:20 hours on the 21st Sergeant Davidson succumbed to his injuries.

Sergeant Murray was transferred to the RAF Hospital at Rauceby. The rest of the crew being listed as "Safe at RAF Station".

Bombing up a Hampden with 250 Pound GP (General Purpose) bombs

Sergeant Davidson was a member of 420 Squadron Royal Canadian Air Force and was originally from Neepawa, Manitoba where he had worked as a Service Station Attendant for the five years prior to joining the Air Force. His parents had emigrated to Canada from Banffshire in Scotland, but he had been born in Canada. Twenty five years-old, he was married to Florence.

Leading Aircraftman Joseph Henry Boucher

Died 7th May 1943

Joseph Boucher is not thought to have ever been based at RAF Waddington, but was instead returned home to his village following his death on another unit. Joseph had moved to Waddington to live with his extended family at an early age, giving rise to the possibility that he had been orphaned.

Following his death in May 1943 in the Shaftesbury Military Hospital in Dorset a post mortem found that he had died of Status Thymico Lymphaticus. Today, this is no longer recognised as a condition, but back then it was used to explain a variety of otherwise unexplained deaths. Cot Death, Sudden Adult Death Syndrome and deaths whilst under anaesthetic were all attributed to Status Thymico Lymphaticus.

With such a wide range of possibilities, few conclusions can be drawn from the Coroner's verdict, except to say that it is likely that Joseph was an outwardly healthy man who died in unexpected circumstances. Military hospitals can have a wide catchment area, so although it is likely he was serving somewhere in the south-west, it is presently impossible to say with any more accuracy what his unit was.

As a previous resident of Waddington Village, it is hoped that more information about Joseph's life will be forthcoming following publication and can feature in future re-prints.

This was the last Second World War burial in St Michael's Churchyard. The station closed between May and October 1943 for new concrete runways to be built. Any further burials would have gone to the Regional Cemeteries.

Corporal Horace Edgar Stacey

Died 17th September 1945

RAF Halton in Buckinghamshire was for many years the home of the RAF's Boy Apprentices, affectionately known as Trenchard's Brats. Even today, it remains one of the RAF's biggest training facilities and as such holds a special place in many airmen's hearts.

It is not known in what capacity Corporal Stacey served at RAF Halton, but on the 16th September 1945, he was walking with a companion down Maitland Road, which runs from the accommodation area towards the main entrance to RAF Halton. Tragically, he was struck by an RAF utility vehicle and suffered severe head injuries from which he was to later die in Princess Mary's Hospital at RAF Halton .

At an inquest held on 21st September 1945, HM Coroner Stanley E Wilkins certified the death due to *"Middle Meningeal Haemorrhage and cerebral contusions following a depressed linear skull fracture caused by the deceased being knocked down on 16th September 1945 at Maitland Road, Halton by an RAF Utility Motor Van"*. A verdict of Misadventure was entered.

Corporal Stacey lived with his wife in Heath Road, Bracebridge Heath, Lincoln and had served for seven years, making him a pre-war entrant. Although it is not known if he had served at RAF Waddington, he was returned home to be buried near where he had lived. He received a military funeral from the station.

Flight Lieutenant Raymond Henry Knight
Navigator II Morris Guy Waterfall
Signaller II James Whitecross Adamson

Died 15th July 1949

The Avro Lincoln was a development of the famous Lancaster, which despite first taking to the air in June 1944, never actually saw active service in World War II. The Lincoln was so closely related to the Lancaster that at first it had been called the Lancaster IV, but eventually the manufacturers decided that the changes were sufficient to justify designating it as a completely new aircraft type.

The Lincoln was bigger than the Lancaster in both length and wingspan. It also benefited from supercharged Rolls Royce Merlin 85 engines. These improvements gave the Lincoln a greater range, a higher operational ceiling and a larger bomb-load than its predecessor. Although just too late for World War II, the Lincoln did eventually see active service in both Kenya and Malaya.

For the crew of RF471, a 61 Squadron Lincoln based at Waddington, this should have been a routine training flight. The weather was not great, with solid cloud above 600 feet, but it was still suitable for the planned instrument flying exercise and shouldn't have presented any problems. However, only 10 minutes after their 14:00 hours take-off, the aircraft was seen to emerge from the low cloud base. At first it appeared to be flying normally, but it suddenly pitched nose-down and dived nearly vertically into the ground near Skellingthorpe.

Avro Lincoln RF394 at Waddington. in March 1949

71

Kurt Patzig, a former prisoner of war who had remained in Lincolnshire at the end of hostilities, was working on Menson Farm, Jerusalem and had a narrow escape when the plane crashed only 100 yards away from him. Later, he was able to give the following account of events:

"I was on my way to fetch a herd of cows, when I heard the plane. It circled the field three times, but I could not see it because of the clouds. It flew off eventually, but returned immediately and when I saw it come out of the clouds it was all on fire. It crashed down behind a hedge and exploded."

The Lincoln Fire Brigade happened to be dealing with a heath fire nearby, but even their rapid intervention was too late to save the crew of seven who had all been killed instantly. They were later assisted by a second pump from Lincoln and the RAF Waddington fire and rescue services.

Although Kurt remembered seeing the aircraft on fire before the crash, it is by no means certain that it was. When witnesses see a traumatic event such as an air crash at close hand, their mind can play tricks on them by trying to explain what they have just seen. As they witness the crash, their subconscious is telling them that aircraft don't just fall out of the sky for no reason and it fills the gaps, more often than not with a fire.

Even in air crashes today, witnesses will often state that they saw the aircraft on fire before the crash. However, the investigation will later positively establish that there was no in flight fire.

An RAF investigation at the time had great difficulty establishing the cause of this accident, not least because the aircraft had been almost completely destroyed. However, they were able to establish that there was no evidence of structural failure or of a fire in the air. The investigation focused on two main possibilities. At first, it was thought possible that a technical failure had caused the pilot to lose control, but in the end the most likely cause seemed to be that the pilot had become disorientated whilst trying to fly by referencing both visual clues and his instruments. This explanation gained greater credence when it was later found that the pilot did not have a current instrument rating.

This sad event came only a day after RAF Waddington had been given the honour of hosting a visit for the Iraqi Regent, a close ally at the time. The whole station had taken part in this visit, but only days later they would assemble again at St Michael's Church to bury three of the crew. The other four crew members were returned home for burial, each escorted on their journey by an officer from 61 Squadron.

RAF Waddington crash rescue service in 1949.

Also killed were: Pilot Officer Robert Ratcliffe(Pilot). Gunner II Clarence Brett (Air Gunner), Gunner I Frederick Searle (Air Gunner) and Engineer I Gerald McCarthy (Air Engineer). The ranks of Gunner I, Signaller II etc. were a short lived trial. Only the rank of Master Aircrew remains of this experiment in today's Royal Air Force.

Pilot ll Patrick Turner
Navigator ll Albert Henry James Mitchell
Signaller l John Edwin Conway Simpson
Gunner ll Ernest Frank Tester
Gunner ll Edward Charles Talbot
Gunner ll Philip Edward Pattullo

Died 26th September 1949

Exercise Bulldog was a major Bomber Command Exercise running from the 23rd to the 26th of September 1949. Less than six months earlier, on 4th April 1949, the North Atlantic Treaty had been signed, marking the formation of NATO (North Atlantic Treaty Organisation). NATO had been formed as a response to the growing threat from the communist armies to the east and the cooling in relations between the two great powers, that was to become known as the Cold War.

The funeral of the three aircrew who were buried with Full Military Honours

It was recognised that no one country could hope to stand alone against the overwhelming numbers of the Soviet Union's Red Army and it was for this reason that western countries had formed a defensive pact in the guise of NATO. Bulldog provided an early opportunity to test how this defensive pact would work, with forces from the United States, Belgium, Holland and France joining the RAF for the four days of the exercise.

Bulldog was an offensive exercise, testing Bomber Command's ability to mount long range strike missions in the face of stiff enemy fighter resistance. Avro Lancasters, Avro Lincolns and Boeing B29 Superfortresses were pitted against the cutting edge jet fighters of the day, the Meteor and Vampire. The exercise had been scheduled to start on the Friday, but bad weather caused this to be delayed until 13:00 hours on the Saturday. On the first mission, bombers simultaneously raided targets across the whole country, including London, Leicester, Reading, Oxford and Gloucester. Despite the late start, this high operational tempo continued and by the evening of 26th September a successful exercise was drawing to a close.

As the crews of two Waddington based Avro Lincolns, RE374 and RF407 approached their target, the newly constructed power station at Staythorpe near Newark, all attention on board must have been fully focused on making their last attack of the exercise as successful as possible. Unbeknown to either crew, their aircraft were closing through the darkness on a converging course.

It will never be known why the aircraft collided, but it was thought at the time that either a thirty second error in timings, poor lookout or last minute evasion to avoid a fighter attack were the most likely culprits. However the Air Officer Commanding concluded that the most likely cause was convergence of the two aircraft rather than poor lookout and this was a matter which was being actively addressed.

The force of the collision, which killed all 14 crew instantly, was witnessed by Flight Lieutenant Michael Thomas Bartlett, a Navigator of 61 Squadron who also airborne that night: *"I was flying on Operation Bulldog, the object of the exercise was to simulate bombing attacks near Newark. The attack was timed for 9.48pm. "My plane got over the target at 16,200 feet and then I saw a very vivid flash behind me which lit up the whole countryside. It appeared to come from slightly lower than our height, each aircraft had been allocated a height for flying over the target."*

Flight Sergeant A Munn of RAF Marham in Norfolk who was on duty at

Staythorpe Power Station also witnessed the collision: *"I did not see any lights of any kind from the aircraft. At 9.36pm I saw a flash in the sky directly over the target. It was at a great height but I did not hear the sound of the actual collision. I later heard an explosion, I did not see any parachutes."*

The Operations Record Book, recorded by Flight Lieutenant F. Ridgeway reads as follows and records the unit's shock at losing 14 men in an instant:

Operation "Bulldog" described as Bomber Command's own exercise, took place during the latter days of this month and a maximum effort of aircraft from the three squadrons of this station participated on the two nights when weather made the attacks practicable. "Bulldog" involved the attacking of targets in Great Britain both by day and night and covering the period 23rd to 27th September. Tasks for the nights of 23/24th September and 24/25th September (Southampton and London) were cancelled and operations took place on the nights of 25/26th September and 26/27th September (Stoke on Trent and Newark). It was at the culmination of the attack on Newark that an accident occurred when two aircraft 57 "H" and 61 "S" collided and crashed. All the occupants of the machines were killed - a total of fourteen. At the time of writing this diary a Court of Inquiry is sitting to attempt to ascertain the cause of this shocking and tragic accident.

Those who died in the two aircraft were: (* Indicates buried in St Michael's Churchyard, Waddington).

Navigator ll Mitchell

From Lincoln RE374 of 57 Squadron: Pilot ll James William Dagger, Engineer l James Sabin, Navigator lll Frederick Hughes, Signaller ll Raymond Charles Wonnacott, Gunner l Stanley Wilson, Pilot ll Patrick Turner*and Gunner ll Ernest Frank Tester.*

From Lincoln RF407 of 61 Squadron: Pilot ll Henry Richardson, Flight Lieutenant John Shorthouse, Engineer ll Charles Denis Kirby, Gunner ll Edward Charles Talbot,* Navigator ll Albert Henry James Mitchell,* Signaller l John Edwin Conway Simpson* and Gunner ll Philip Edward Pattullo.*

The funerals took place at Waddington on Friday 30th September where the six air crew were afforded Full Military Honours. All the others were returned to their homes for a private funeral, each being accompanied by an officer representing the Commanding Officer. Air Vice Marshal Mills who was at the station to witness Exercise Bulldog attended the Waddington funerals.

In March 2013, Mrs Olive Tasker, formerly Mrs Olive Mitchell, the wife of Albert Mitchell, re-visited RAF Waddington where she had been a member of the WAAF when she married. On hearing of the preparation of this book she kindly wrote about her memories of her husband, the funeral and her life in its aftermath.

'I came to meet "Mitch" Mitchell as he was always known, in the Lincoln NAAFI club. He had come to Waddington from Skellingthorpe as a member of 61 Squadron - a man always full of life, enthusiasm and always with a cheery smile. He loved his service life as did I and we married having a son together, Ian James.

Life at Waddington was a wonderful time & I loved my work at the station HQ on the switchboard both day & night. My times in the service there were amongst the happiest of my young life and of course meeting Mitch. Many evenings were spent in the NAAFI club chatting with friends and drinking endless cups of tea or coffee. There was also the station cinema, aptly called "The Astra", although no film was taken seriously with the noisy audience whistling, cheering & booing every film.

The village of Waddington was quite different then (1946), a real village with narrow lanes and old flint walls. I recall an elderly gentleman who baked in an old style stone oven known locally as "Pop". We would often stroll back from the village eating one of "Pops" pies straight from the oven. On my recent visit to the station the years rolled back and I found it so nostalgic to see the still familiar buildings even though so much has changed.

For Mitch, he enjoyed every moment of his life at Waddington, and also served in the Canal Zone, Shallufa, & Cyprus. At the time of Operation Bulldog he was preparing for an upcoming 12 week posting to Australia, although I never knew the purpose of that posting. Sadly that was never to be, as he along with 13 other crew were killed in the mid air collision between two Lincoln bombers during operation Bulldog flying under wartime conditions on the evening of 26th September 1949. One aircraft from 61 Sqn, the other from 57 Sqn came down at Staythorpe near Newark.

As his wife I was devastated and left with a baby boy and with some harsh realities to face up to. The fact that Mitch would never see him grow into the

Olive Mitchell

fine young man he became. The sadness didn't end there, as Ian too lost his life in a road traffic accident at the age of 20, just two weeks before he was due to follow his father's footsteps into the RAF. It has been a daily heartbreak since.

I clearly remember the funeral service at St. Michael's and hearing a speaker say "It is the price we have to pay". I am certain I was not the only one there to think the price was much too high.

I re-married 4 years later having a second son, Robert who has been my rock since his father passed away several years ago. We both have enjoyed our very privileged visit to Waddington though and visited St Michael's Churchyard where Mitch is buried alongside other crew members.

His parents gave their blessing to my decision that he should be buried there due to his love of the service and Waddington in particular. It was also very poignant to visit the memorial garden on station which is a fitting tribute to all those who lost their lives - God bless them all.'

As if this tragedy wasn't enough, Exercise Bulldog was credited with another Waddington fatality on 28th September when an airman, who had been engaged in tractor driving at the Bomb Dump as part of the exercise, was found dead beside his upturned tractor at a bend in the perimeter track.

At the subsequent inquest the South Lincoln Coroner, Major W P Pattinson, recorded a verdict of Accidental Death on 19 year old Aircraftman II Hadyn Gilmore Morgan, whose home was in Swansea.

The papers reported that no one saw the accident, but that Morgan had died of a fractured skull. Warrant Officer Leslie Hollingsworth gave evidence that Morgan was a somewhat erratic driver and he had spoken to him earlier about his driving.

He went on to say that he had been drawing trolleys for Exercise Bulldog and was about to put the tractor away when the accident happened. He was taking a hairpin bend when the tractor went over. He was returned home for burial.

The above and next 3 pictures show the funeral of the six airmen

Flight Sergeant J H Brown

Died 11th April 1951

Flight Sergeant Brown was described as a very popular member of 57 Squadron's Technical Wing. Although at present little is known of his RAF career, he had been on detachment with the squadron to Singapore from March to June 1950. He died of natural causes after a long illness whilst under the care of the military hospital at Wroughton in Wiltshire. He was buried with Full Military Honours. Aged only 34, he left a wife and three children.

Flight Sergeant Brown's coffin is moved to waiting transport on the station

Above: Flight Sergeant Brown's funeral procession leaves RAF Waddington
Below: the coffin is carried into the Churchyard

The internment of Flight Sergeant Brown at St Michael's Churchyard. Note the wooden crosses showing the graves of those from the previously described funeral almost 18 months earlier and before the stone grave markers had been installed.

Squadron Leader Albert Edward Gamble
Squadron Leader Edward John Eames AFC
Squadron Leader James George Woodgate Stroud

Died 1st October 1956

Vulcan XA897 was the first of its type to enter Squadron service with the RAF. It arrived at RAF Waddington on 20th July 1956 and became 230 Operational Conversion Unit's first aircraft. The role of 230 Operational Conversion Unit was to train qualified pilots to fly the Vulcan, no mean task given the completely revolutionary design of Britain's newest nuclear bomber.

XA897 soon had to return to the factory at Woodford for routine modifications, but by September it was back at Waddington and ready to set out on an epic journey to Australia and New Zealand, which was to go under the name Operation Tasman Flight. This was not just an opportunity for the RAF to show off their latest cutting-edge hardware, at this stage there were also very real hopes that Australia and New Zealand might be export customers for the Vulcan.

Air Marshal Sir Harry Broadhurst

The aircraft left Boscombe Down on 9th September, planning to route via Aden and Singapore. On board were two additional crew members, Mr F Bassett a civilian engineer from Avro and Air Marshal Sir Harry Broadhurst who at that time was Air Officer Commander in Chief of Bomber Command.

On arrival in Singapore, Air Marshal Broadhurst told reporters: *"The aircraft behaved perfectly on the trip from Great Britain. The flight from the United Kingdom to Aden took seven hours fifteen minutes and from Aden to Singapore eight hours six minutes. One significant factor of the flight was that it shows the Vulcan can move immense power from one side of the world to the other very quickly. I am quite sure that this aircraft is just as good as anything the Russians or the United States of America might have"*

Air Marshal Broadhurst had a distinguished career as a fighter pilot in World War II and unusually for a senior officer, he continued to fly operationally shooting down a confirmed 13 enemy aircraft with a further 7 classified as probables. By 1942 he was the youngest ever Air Marshal and was leading the RAF's Desert Air Force.

A Waddington Vulcan readies for a prestige overseas visit alongside two other icons of the era, the Comet and the Britannia.

XA 897 in Australia

The Vulcan was not like any bomber that preceeded it. It's fighter like performance would require a new mindset and this was why Broadhurst, with his fighter pilot background, was brought in to lead Bomber Command.

At around 17:00 hours on the 11th September, the Vulcan arrived at Royal Australian Air Force Station Avalon near Melbourne. For the next few days, Air Marshal Broadhurst was engaged in diplomatic and ceremonial duties, but managed to temporarily embroil himself in controversy by insulting Australia's latest fighter, the Avon Sabre.

The Avon Sabre was an Australian built version of the famous North American F86 Sabre. At first, Broadhurst told the press that *"The Sabre was well suited to its task when first built, but has been completely outdated by recent developments"* implying that the Vulcan was not vulnerable to attack from Australia's latest fighter. He later had to retract this and tried to save face by stating that he had been talking about night-time and that the fact that the Sabre was not a night-fighter. The rest of the trip, including a visit to New Zealand went without a hitch.

Early on the morning of the 1st October the Vulcan departed Christchurch for the transit home. The journey was uneventful and all that remained was to land at London Heathrow Airport for a VIP reception.

As the Vulcan approached the south coast, the captain, Squadron Leader Donald Howard contacted Bomber Command Operations and was informed of poor weather at Heathrow. The cloud was solid down to 800 feet and it only fully cleared at 300 feet, but even then there was heavy rain below. He was also informed that the weather at Waddington was good. Howard radioed back that he would make one attempt to land at Heathrow before diverting to Waddington.

This was not an unreasonable decision as most airliners were landing normally at Heathrow, with the exception of three Russian Tupolev Tu104s which were bringing the Bolshoi Ballet to London, who had diverted to nearby RAF Manston where the weather was much better.

Howard elected to make a Ground Controlled Approach, known as a GCA. In this type of approach, the air traffic controller looks at two radar scopes. The first sweeps left and right across a small arc, a line marks the correct approach path and the controller gives instructions to turn left or right as appropriate to maintain on the extended centre line of the runway. The second scope sweeps up and down through a similarly small arc and shows the aircraft's position relative to the glide slope. The glide slope is a gently descending path which meets the ground at the runway threshold. Using the information from these two scopes, the ground controller is able to talk the pilot down onto the runway in poor weather.

An important part of this process is the pilot's decision as to what height he will descend to before breaking-off the approach, this is known as the decision height. Whilst on the approach, the pilot is flying on instruments. Once he reaches his decision height, he looks up. If he sees the runway ahead of him, he lands. If not, he applies full power and climbs away. Crucially, Howard selected a decision height of just 300 feet.

Howard's approach to the airport was relatively normal. There were some significant divergences from the ideal path, but he managed to correct these. It was certainly nothing that alarmed his co-pilot Air Marshal Broadhurst. Broadhurst's job as co-pilot was to monitor the approach and look out for the first sign of the runway lights. At ¾ of a mile from touchdown the controller gave the last part of the talk-down, informing the pilot that he was 80 feet high. The recording of the radar picture would later show that the aircraft entered a steep descent and struck the ground seven seconds later.

Contrary to what was recorded on the radar picture, the aircraft struck the ground with only a glancing blow. The pilot then applied full power with the intention of climbing away and diverting to Waddington. It soon became apparent though, that the aircraft was mortally wounded. When Howard found that he was unable to correct the aircraft's roll to the right he realised that the controls had been damaged and was forced to eject. Broadhurst first tried the controls himself and upon finding them unresponsive, he too ejected. Unbeknown to them, the undercarriage had been forced backwards on its hinge, severing the control rods to the ailerons. The ailerons are the control surface which controls the aircraft in roll.

The chaotic scenes at Heathrow Airport as the Vulcan fires rage

Squadron Leader Howard later described these events at the inquiry: *"I asked the co-pilot to look for the high intensity lighting which I was going to use for the landing. He told me he could see the lights over to starboard, and all this time I was looking at instruments and not looking out. I looked at the lights as he told me, and I did not recognise the pattern. They were not what I expected to see. Immediately I had looked I went back to instruments and he then told me I was very low and to pull up and so I did. At that precise time the aeroplane touched the ground and I decided to overshoot. This I tried to do, but as the aircraft accelerated it became obvious that I could not control it any more. It wanted to roll over to the right. I used all the control I had but I could not stop it. My altimeter was showing slightly less than 300 feet. I shouted to the crew to get out and when it was apparent the aircraft was going to roll into the ground, I decided to eject."*

Squadron Leader Howard photographed immediately after the crash

A poor reproduction of a picture of the crew, but the best we can achieve. It shows them on arrival at Avalon, Australia having flown England-Aden-Singapore-Melbourne. Left to right: Mr Frederick Bassett, civilian engineer for the manufacturers of the Vulcan, A V Roe, Squadron Leader Eames (Navigator), Squadron Leader Howard (Pilot and Captain), Squadron Leader Stroud (Pilot acting as Navigator) and Squadron Leader Gamble (Air Electronics Officer).

Air Marshal Broadhurst also gave evidence: *"The talk-down was normal, there was nothing in it to alarm you. It seemed perfectly safe. After hitting the ground with a glancing blow I was convinced that no damage had been done and even commented that if we turn slightly left we can still make it."*

For the four rear crew, who were not equipped with ejector seats, there was no chance of escape and they were all killed. Broadhurst landed on the runway, injuring his foot in the process and Howard landed on grass adjacent to the runway suffering only a grazed head.

The inquiry focused on the Ground Controlled Approach and the fact that the controller did not warn the crew in the final seconds of their high rate of descent. In many respects, it was convenient for the RAF to lay the blame on an external agency there was much about the accident that could prove very embarrassing.

Aviation accidents are rarely caused by a single failure, they are more often a chain of events which all need to happen together for an accident to occur. In this case, Squadron Leader Stroud, the experienced Vulcan co-pilot had been replaced by Air Marshal Broadhurst. Stroud whose experience might have prevented the accident was sat in the rear of the aircraft.

It was recognised at the time that an altimeter error of 70 feet existed and the pilot had accounted for this. It was later found that as the aircraft approached the ground it could in fact be an error of over 200 feet. For the approach the pilot had selected a break-off height of 300 feet above mean sea-level. Because Heathrow is 80 feet above sea-level, this represents 220 feet above the surface. The pilot applied an altimeter error of 70 feet, meaning that at no point did he expect to be below 150 feet above the surface. However, with an altimeter error of over 200 feet, it is quite possible that he struck the ground with an altimeter that was telling him he was at 300 feet. The pressure to land at Heathrow must have been immense for Squadron Leader Howard with one of the most senior officers in the RAF sat in the seat next to him. Although he was the captain, in reality it was very difficult for him to say he was not going to try and land at Heathrow and ruin the Air Marshal's VIP reception.

Over fifty years have elapsed since this accident and we will probably never know the precise cause, but a mixture of human factors and unknown errors within the altimeter seem likely. The accident remained a mystery for Air Marshal Broadhurst too: *"The whole thing is a puzzle to me. It seemed to me an absolutely normal glide approach until the ground appeared in the wrong place. If we had been coming down at an unprecedented rate we would have hit the ground and the undercarriage would have been forced up into the wings. As it was we touched so lightly that we merely thought the aircraft had burst a tyre or something."*

As well as the military losing three highly qualified and experienced officers in this tragic crash, A V Roe and Co. Ltd (Avro) lost one of their leading technicians. The one civilian on board, Mr Frederick Bassett was 32 years of age and had joined the Royal Air Force straight from school, leaving as a Corporal Fitter in 1945. He was then employed by Avro as a fitter in the experimental department and in 1950 was promoted to inspector in the technical services department. It was as the company's technical expert on the Vulcan that he was chosen to go on the flight to Australia.

The funerals of the three servicemen took place at St Michael's Church on Friday 5th October. The service was conducted by Reverend W R G Pellant (Station Chaplain) and the Reverend J N Keeling (Assistant Chaplain in Chief, Bomber Command). The Air Officer Commanding No 1 Group, Bomber Command, Air Vice Marshal G A Walker CBE, DSO, DFC, AFC attended the service with many other officers from the station and elsewhere. The church was packed for the service. The coffins of the three officers were laid side by side. They were then buried with Full Military Honours. Pictures of funeral follow.

Senior Officers and fellow officers from Waddington pay their respects at the gravesides.

Sergeant Richard William Priestly
Died 13th December 1956

Nocton Hall, in the village of Nocton, just south-east of Lincoln was requisitioned by the Air Ministry in 1940. It became an RAF Hospital and remained as such until its closure in 1984.

It was briefly reactivated for the First Gulf War by the United States Air Force in 1990, but in the event, mercifully, few casualties passed through its doors. Today, this beautiful building lies in ruins following an arson attack, but locals are still hopeful that it will eventually rise from the ashes.

Sergeant Priestly had been admitted to RAF Hospital Nocton Hall, suffering from a recurrent kidney infection. Sadly, doctors were not able to save him and he died of kidney failure.

Corporal George Brian Christison
Died 16th December 1958

Corporal Christison was serving at RAF Yatesbury in Wiltshire, which at the time was the Radar and Wireless Training School. It was quite a primitive base, mostly consisting of wooden huts heated only by a Pot Belly stove, so the opportunity to visit family and sample a few home comforts for a while must have been a welcome one.

George was from Dunfermline in Fife and was on his way home to spend Christmas with his family. Having decided to break his journey, he took the opportunity to spend the weekend with his uncle, Flight Lieutenant William Bridgewood, who was based at RAF Waddington.

With his visit complete, George set-off once again for Dunfermline. The weather was atrocious, with a very persistent, thick fog. Tragically he had barely started his journey before disaster struck. On the Grantham Road, between the entrance to the station and Bracebridge Heath, George's sports car collided head-on wit a lorry belonging to a Lincoln corn merchant.

The station Medical Officer, Flight Lieutenant Chaudoir attended the crash, but there was nothing he could do to save George, who had died at the scene. At the subsequent inquest, it was discovered that he had died of internal injuries.

During his summing-up, the coroner remarked: *"With this fog about you have to be careful. Certain hazards have to be taken such as crossing a road, but in this case it is a straight road."* He later added: *"These things always seem to happen at Christmastime."* Indeed, whilst researching this and other books, it became apparent that the RAF has always suffered an increase in road-traffic casualties at the beginning of holidays such as Christmas and Easter. The desire to get home as quickly as possible to have more time with friends and family, seems to sometimes over-ride the need for safe driving.

This was the last military burial in St Michael's Churchyard.

RAF Waddington Heritage Centre

RAF Waddington has a proud and distinguished history spanning more than 90 years. Following its opening in November 1916 as a flying training base, the Station had aircraft and people involved in both World Wars, including the participation of 44 Squadron in the famous Augsburg bombing raid in 1942. During the Cold War the Station had significant involvement with the Black Buck raids of the Falklands campaign and nowadays all of the aircraft stationed here are involved in operations around the world.

Numerous squadrons have served here and over time a significant number of personnel have donated their prized memorabilia from their time serving in Lincolnshire; this has enabled a small collection to be established in the Station Heritage Centre for all to learn from and enjoy.

The Heritage Centre is a voluntarily run museum which allows you to step into the history of RAF Waddington. The displays will let you travel back in time and engage with this history, from the wreckage of the downed Avro Lancaster PD-259 from WWII through to the Vulcan bomber XM607 of Black Buck fame, which currently stands as the Station's Gate Guardian.

With plenty to see and learn you are sure to leave with a greater knowledge of the Station's standing in past and current operations. Furthermore, they are part of the Aviation Heritage Lincolnshire partnership with links to other museums within the county who are also proud of their aviation heritage.

The centre is now open to all civilians and service personnel on an appointment basis and best of all it's free (although a small donation to enable the upkeep is appreciated). Due to the operational nature of the Station, anyone wishing to book a visit should contact the Visits Co-ordinator or the Officer in Charge of the Heritage Centre via the details below.

For visits or to contact the Heritage Centre at RAF Waddington email:

WAD-Heritagecentre@mod.uk
or alternatively via telephone on:
Officer in Charge Heritage Centre 01522 727367
Officer in Charge Force Development Sqn 01522 727090

Above:A Vulcan flies over Lincoln Cathedral. Below Lancaster bombing up in 1944

Inside the RAF Waddington Heritage Centre

We hope you have enjoyed reading one of our books in the Below the Glide Path series. Should you have any information about anything or anyone mentioned in this or any of the other books, please do not hesitate to contact us. Further copies of this, or our other books, Wings Over York and Slightly Below the Glide Path - RAF Scampton - RAF Digby and RAF Linton on Ouse can also be obtained by contacting the e mail address below.

brian.mennell305@sky.com

High resolution images are always welcome and can be sent to this e mail address or if original photographs are involved please e mail us
to arrange their secure copying

Plan of Military Graves in St Michael's Churchyard, Waddington

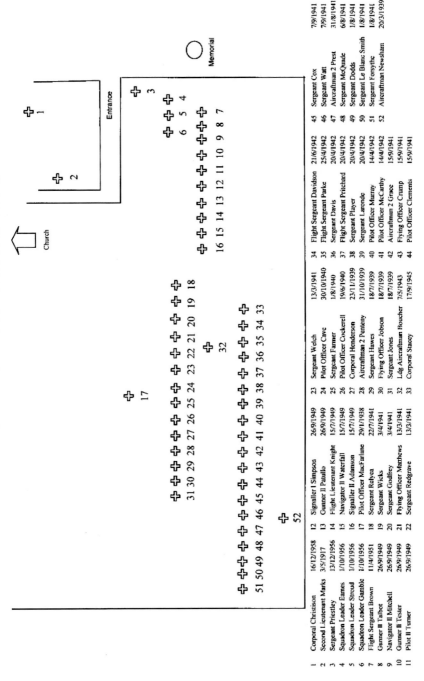

Bibliography

We are indebted to the authors of the following books which assisted and / or enabled us in our research:

Air Force Memorials of Lincolnshire. M. Ingham
An illustrated history of RAF Waddington. Raymond Leach
Bomber Command War Diaries. M. Middlebrook and C. Everitt
Bomber Command War Losses (all). W. R. Chorley
Bomber County. T. N. Hancock
Category Five. Colin Cummings
Fighter Command Losses (all). Norman L. R. Franks
Final Landings. Colin Cummings
Grantham in the news 1926-1950. John Pinchbeck
Hampden Crash Log. Nicholas Roberts
Heroes of Bomber Command, Lincolnshire. Rupert Matthews
Last Take-off. Colin Cummings
Lancaster. Christopher Chant
Lincolnshire Air War. Books 1&2. S. Finn
Luftwaffe Night Fighter Combat Claims 1939 - 1945. John Foreman
Operational Record Books. RAF Waddington via National Archives, Kew
The Hampden File. H. Moyle
The King's Thunderbolts. Alan White
The Price of Peace. Colin Cummings
The Vulcan Story. Tim Laming
They Shall Grow Not Old. L Allison and H Hayward
To Fly no more. Colin Cummings
Waddington at War 1939 - 1941. Terry Miller and Jean Towers

We are further grateful to the following sources of information: The families, friends and acquaintances of those in the cemetery. All those who have contributed accounts and memories. RAF Waddington Heritage Centre. The National Archive, Kew. The Lincolnshire Echo. Lincoln Libraries and their staff, The Station Commander, RAF Waddington. Library and Archives, Ottawa, Canada. RAF Museum, Hendon. RAF Air Historical Branch. Commonwealth War Graves Commission. Registrar of Births Deaths and Marriages, Lincoln.